Praise for *Counterproductive Culture*

"This is the best thing I've read in quite a while. You've hit the nail on the head dead on!"

"Fantastic read! This needs to be required reading of every CEO and leadership team in every industry."

"This is amazing! And so true."

"Can't agree more…when the wrong people are offered power, they misuse it, and talented people leave."

"One of the best and most inspiring…great words here!"

"Absolutely spot on…your perspective brings invaluable insight. Your emphasis on seeking understanding before speaking and sharing praise alongside constructive feedback demonstrates a people-focused approach that's crucial for fostering positive cultures."

"Finally, someone that got it right!"

COUNTERPRODUCTIVE CULTURE

NAVIGATING TODAY'S MODERN WORKFORCE AND HOW
YOUR OLD BUSINESS HABITS ARE THE SABOTEURS OF WORKPLACE SUCCESS

Workplace Press Publishing Co., USA

Copyright © Francesco R. Benzo 2024

All Rights Reserved

© Workplace Press Publishing Co 2024. All rights reserved.

No part of this publication may be reproduced, distributed, or transmitted in any form or by any means, including photocopying, recording, or other electronic or mechanical methods except in the case of brief quotations embodied in critical reviews and certain other noncommercial uses permitted by copyright law.

The information contained in this book is provided for educational and informational purposes only and is not intended as legal, financial, medical, or other professional advice. The author and publisher have made every effort to ensure the accuracy and completeness of the information contained in this book; however, they assume no responsibility for errors, inaccuracies, omissions, or any other inconsistencies herein.

The author and publisher specifically disclaim any liability, loss, or risk, personal or otherwise, which is incurred as a consequence, directly or indirectly, of the use and application of any of the contents of this book. Readers are encouraged to consult a professional where appropriate.

All images, art, photographs and drawings contained within are property and Copyright of Francesco R. Benzo.

First Edition

Contents

Introduction: Energized, Encouraged, Excited, and Emotional 1
Chapter 1: Counterfeit Culture 2
Chapter 2: The First Problem You See Is Not The Root Cause of The Problem 60
Chapter 3: Toxic Positivity 69
Chapter 4: Your D.E.I. Program Needs A Mental Health Check 72
Chapter 5: Stop Looking For Servants 75
Chapter 6: The Fish Rots From The Head 78
Chapter 7: Is Your Apron Dirty? 83
Chapter 8: Work Harder, I Want More! 85
Chapter 9: It's OK, You Can Tell Us 88
Chapter 10: To Bonus Or Not To Bonus? 91
Chapter 11: Your HR Is Disrupted 95
Chapter 12: Coach To Improve, Not Remove 98
Chapter 13: He Who Has The Gold Makes The Rules 104
Chapter 14: We're Looking For Someone Different 112
Chapter 15: Contract Your Way Out 125
Chapter 16: Please, Help Me! 129
Chapter 17: I.T. Is It 133
Chapter 18: Survey Says! 138
Chapter 19: Be Good To Good Vendors 140
Chapter 20: Don't Let The Great Be The Enemy Of The Good 143
Conclusion 146

"In cubicles and offices, where dreams are meant to grow,
A culture toxic festers, and progress moves so slow.
The whispers in the hallways, the gossip in the air,
Create a web of tension, a climate of despair.

Decisions made in shadows, where secrets breed distrust,
The values once held sacred now tarnished and unjust.
The bosses seek their power, their ego as their guide,
While innovation withers, and talent steps aside.

Meetings drone on endless, with little being said,
The vision once so vibrant now lies there cold and dead.
The clock ticks ever louder, as motivation fades,
While workers seek a purpose in murky, shifting shades.

The rigid rules and structures, the fear to take a risk,
Turn agile minds to shackles, a bureaucratic disk.
The passion once ignited now flickers, wanes, and dies,
And all that's left is burnout, beneath the weary skies.

No room for collaboration, for voices to be heard,
Just silos of division, where nothing is preferred.
The feedback loops are broken, the growth is kept at bay,
And in this stale environment, the best will walk away.

For in a culture toxic, where bad habits hold their reign,
The cost is not just profit, but innovation's gain.
The brightest minds will falter, the stars will dim their light,
And what could be a beacon, will vanish in the night.

So heed this humble warning, let kindness pave the way,
For healthy, thriving workplaces will see a brighter day.
Embrace the voice of many, let teamwork be your creed,
And watch as your endeavor fulfills each noble need.

For in the heart of business, where cultures rise and fall,
The key to true success is the well-being of all." - *FRB*

INTRODUCTION

ENERGIZED, ENCOURAGED, EXCITED, AND EMOTIONAL

The knowledge, experiences, education, and content in this book are meant to open the eyes and ears of those who have or are looking to build, maintain, and contribute to running a successful business. If you find yourself energized, encouraged, and excited by the words that follow, this likely means you have participated in the healthy and productive behaviors I've suggested—and have seen your business or workplace benefit from it. Contrarily, if you find yourself upset, disagreeing with, or even angered by my words, I conclude that, on some occasions, you have been a part of the negative behaviors I describe in this book, *Counterproductive Culture*—and you need to make a change. And that's quite all right! None of us are perfect. Mistakes are made. However, within every one of us is room for genuine improvement. So read on with confidence, acknowledging that by opening this book you've already made a commitment to yourself, to your business, and to the people you lead. Enjoy, learn, and grow. May we all be much improved by the time you make it to the back cover.

Francesco R. Benzo

1
COUNTERFEIT CULTURE

From 2002 to 2016, Wells Fargo was revered as one of the best places to work. They were recognized multiple times as a premier employer and even won the Optimas Award for General Excellence. Behind the scenes, however, things were not as presented to the general public. The top executives were pressuring employees to meet impossible goals, and even though they boasted of a great work culture, the truth was quite the opposite. Frantic and desperate to meet lofty and unrealistic goals, their workplace culture was as toxic as black mold.

What happened next was unbelievable. Succumbing to their employer's demands, employees began to open more than 2 million fake accounts to meet their goals. You read that right! If a customer opened a checking account, an employee of Wells Fargo might open a savings account or credit card in that same customer's name without their knowledge. They called this "upselling" but forgot to tell the customer they were selling it!

Wells Fargo's profits soared to a high of almost 90 billion until they were caught in 2016. Wells Fargo ended up having to pay over 2 billion in fines to the SEC and Department of Justice. The question is, with such an already immensely successful company, why did those within Wells Fargo decide to take a shortcut and a dishonest path to achieve the goals set forth before them? The answer is simple, greed.

Counterproductive Culture

While everyone wants to grow their business, many times business owners are blinded by initial success and forget that you can only grow so fast. With this loss of positive vision comes greed and a desire to have everything instantly, resulting in unreasonable goals for growth.

You see, there is no greater demotivator to your employees than demanding they meet unachievable or even impossible goals to continue your company's growth. At some point, the negative pressure will result in your workforce taking shortcuts to try and meet the pie-in-the-sky end result. This leads us to our topic.

Perhaps one of the greatest indicators of a productive and efficient workplace is a positive company culture. While this is no secret, it's surprising how many organizations fall short in this regard. Commonly, companies will boast about how great their workplace culture is, but when it comes time to walk the talk, they run in the opposite direction or, step right on top of you. I call this a *counterfeit culture*. So many times, business owners and leaders know their workplace culture falls short, yet they continue to pretend and shout to the rooftops as if it's up to par.

Here are the common areas where a company's culture falls short and becomes counterfeit:

- Atmosphere
- Autonomy
- Training
- Leadership
- Acceptable workload
- Vacation and work-life balance

Now, let's break these down:

Atmosphere. Do you have a "put your head down and work" vibe going on? Employees are looking for a place where they are not afraid to voice an opinion, point something out, or talk out loud about ideas. If there is any type of fear in the atmosphere, your company is sending the wrong message and turnover will likely increase dramatically.

The environment needs to not only be open, but honest. How can you expect your employees to provide their ideas and experiences in an environment that really doesn't want to hear them? With the amount of dedication required today, everyone deserves to work somewhere that is honest, transparent, and not only listens but acts upon every single idea or experience had.

We need to think less about our employees' roles in our companies as positions and more about them as human beings. For instance, what does your company do for its people to help them

Counterproductive Culture

unwind and develop more as an individual? Do you ever pull your people away even for just one day to help refresh their minds, or do you keep them at the grind, requiring them to be available 24/7 for any call on your whim?

I encourage everyone to think about this. Think about activities that can help your people get refreshed, feel appreciated, build teamwork, and help them learn new skills that benefit their personal growth. When planning activities, make sure you offer a variety that your team can choose from. Blocking them into an activity they really don't want to do can be detrimental, and counterproductive.

As an example, not everyone can go rock climbing or on outdoor adventures together. Going out to dinner for "team drinks" is likely also not something all of your employees would want to do. Forcing your employees into an activity they don't want to participate in will cause further team deterioration and eventually, turnover. Thinking of ideas for team activities is really as simple as *asking* your team what *they* would like to do. Do *they* want to go on a hike? Do *they* want to have a painting class? Do *they* want to have a book day or present their hobbies to everyone? Do *they* want you to roll a giant TV into the office for a day to watch a show? What do *they* want to do?

You see, you need to take their minds away from your business in order for them to refocus on it! If there's stress in your environment, team exercises that have nothing to do with your business are the exact type of thing that can get people back together and working positively. A stressful environment can be like having writers' block. No matter how hard your people try to solve problems, there is so much stress that they cannot see the correct solution. Breaking your team away from the daily grind for even one day can provide you, your employees, and your business with a huge benefit. Do something for them where they can all easily participate together and feel more compelled to do so.

To foster a positive atmosphere, people also need to feel seen and heard. When someone tries to speak with you, stop what you're doing and speak with them. If you can't make time to speak with your employees, they won't make time for you when someone is needed to come in early or stay late. The idea makers will disappear. And although it might seem obvious, when someone does something nice for you and helps you, say *thank you*! Basic *manners* go a very long way.

Another thing that contributes greatly to atmosphere is organization—or lack thereof. Organization is the key to success. Not just for you but for your entire team. In a controlled and organized environment, it's easy for everyone to maintain self-control and organization. In an uncontrolled and unorganized environment, those who typically struggle to maintain self-control will stick to their own routine as no structure is being provided for them in which they can learn from.

If your leadership team is unorganized, you will find they pile things on desks like hoarders, they do not plan, fail to create basic schedules, do not meet deadlines, take forever to make decisions, and do not communicate on a frequent basis. They even fail to do things as simple as returning phone calls and emails. Because of this, you will turn people over non-stop. Don't forget, you require all of these things from your people so, your people should be able to require them of you as the employer, too. What type of controlled structure are you providing for your team members? Highly organized? Well-planned? Communicates frequently? Ask yourself these questions and remember, your people will respect an organized culture.

Autonomy. Micromanaging builds distrust. Employees want communication but don't want to be micromanaged to the point where they feel like someone is holding their hand and is tying their shoes for them. Micromanaging is prodding. Prodding becomes pushing and pushing is negative motivation. When you push people for goals versus achieving them through positive motivation, knowledge, and support, your people tune you out. When your people tune you out, they go and get a new job, just like changing the channel on a TV. They no longer want to watch you and pick another show to invest their time in. Jobs are everywhere and everyone is hiring.

Here are a few things leaders should avoid when trying to change the perception of autonomy in the workplace:

- Too many inspections and surprise visits.
- Overly evaluating your staff.
- Too many surveys and constantly asking for surveys to get done.
- Too many meetings to "communicate".

All of these things can quickly become a *point of perception* where employees feel distrusted, micromanaged, and fearful. Think about updating your routines and showing more confidence in your team members. Encourage your team to provide you with communication on their goal status instead of always asking them or requiring them to be in meetings to tell you. Lighten up on the points above. If you're doing these things, you're driving your people nuts.

Training. Employees often feel they are investing their lives to help someone else's business. With this, they are looking for an employer to not only develop their on-the-job skills but also help them with personal growth that includes continuous, tangible education which can be beneficial for them in all life cycles. Teach your people skills they can use themselves rather than a skill only meant for your business. On-the-job skills are great, however, when you teach an employee a personal skill, it helps keep their mind focused on your business, too. Why? Because you helped them be better and as human beings, we are programmed to give back. We take care of those who take care of us.

You want your employees to make money for you. But, in trying to make money, do you push your employees backward or do you move them forward with exceptional life training that can be applied everywhere?

Leadership and an acceptable workload. Employees expect to see leadership handling the same measure of workload and work schedule that they're given. Your employees understand that all levels of management will have different responsibilities. It is, however, no longer acceptable for companies to have dozens of different Vice Presidents and Executives who stay in the corporate office staring through glass all day long. I call these executives *Vice Presidents in charge of looking out the window!* Employees expect to see all levels of leadership, even ownership, on the ground working side by side every single day. Gone are the days of leadership skipping out to play golf. How can you request someone to work hard if you aren't doing the same?

Vacation and Work-Life Balance. Providing a quality-of-life balance for your employees is also essential. Your employees spend more time with you than with their own families. You should invest as much in your employees as possible. After all, they are investing their lives with you. *What is an employee's life worth to you?* It sounds like a harsh statement but, think about it. You are indeed paying for them to spend their time and a huge part of their life with you.

Did you know many employees are far more interested in the ability to have one more week of paid vacation time versus having a high-potential bonus program? Did you know that when many employees look to change jobs, they're looking for more vacation time versus a higher salary?

Francesco R. Benzo

Rested employees are focused and more productive employees! Health concerns are still everywhere, and family time is extremely important. Remember, your employees spend more time working with you than they do with their own families. Dangling a huge bonus potential bonus in front of someone doesn't have the impact it used to.

Two weeks of paid vacation no longer cuts it either, especially if there is a long waiting time before having the ability to take them. If you're trying to sell 2 weeks of vacation time after 1 year of service, you're going to fall short with every single potential employee. Would you accept a job where you had to wait an entire year before you were allowed to schedule even one vacation day? The answer is no, you wouldn't.

"*Little Silvio – Work-Life Balance*"

Giving one more week of vacation (from 2 to 3 or 3 to 4) should not be an investment that is overlooked. That one week's extra paycheck will return itself in the form of better performance, improved numbers, and a lower turnover rate! It also gains you a lot of appreciation from your people.

Replacing a lost employee can cost 1.5 to 2 times that employee's salary. Having a great employee 48 or 49 out of 52 weeks is far better than losing them to another employer who provides that improved vacation plan. What has your company done to improve its vacation plan and other benefits, aside from increasing salary? Offering a healthy and robust vacation plan is a make-it-or-break-it for most of the workforce at this point.

In fact, many companies are moving to an automatic minimum 3-week paid vacation plan paired with 5 personal days, totaling 4 weeks of time. This is on top of a small handful of sick days for when someone is ill. Many companies see this as a positive to not only attract but also keep great employees working for them. Company leaders who manage from the bottom line up may see this as an investment they cannot afford, however, ask yourself this: If you invested even 1 more week of vacation with an employee that you lost—would they have stayed? In many cases, the answer will be "Yes, they would have stayed if we offered more vacation. It would have given them the chance to reset and spend time with their families." While you're paying for another week, you also just saved yourself far more money because you kept someone happy and under your employ. Now, you don't have to hire and invest in training a new employee. Don't forget,

Counterproductive Culture

when you lose an experienced person, production also declines, resulting in a loss of sales and performance on the bottom line.

You should have vacation available immediately. Companies having the best success hiring are matching existing vacation plans the prospective employee has with their current employer or are offering theirs to be scheduled during the very first year. As we already discussed, candidates who must wait one full year to earn and take any vacation will most likely not be interested in joining your team. If they take the job, they'll end up quitting the second they can land a better role. These are the simplest things to think about and it is not difficult to put a cost to the vacation investment versus the hiring and retraining investment. If you have this opportunity, give it a try. Your people will *thank* you for it.

Work-life balance isn't just important, it's required. This is a non-negotiable for today's working generation. It's not the fault of the newer working generations that they "don't want to work." It's the fault of the previous generations for accepting that they would have to work all the time to make ends meet and would rarely be with their families. Today's working generation grew up having their parents miss nearly every sporting event, and every choir and musical performance. They grew up watching their parents having to work every single weekend and watched them be dissatisfied with their lives. In growing up with this, today's working generation has demanded a change. It's not always about *money*. More frequently, it's about treatment and balance. Does your team really need to spend 6 days a week working for you? Does your team really need to spend 55 to 60 hours, or more, working with you every week? If they do, your business is broken, or your goals are unrealistic. The scale doesn't need to be tipped all the way to either side. It simply needs to be even. Making it even doesn't mean giving someone a bonus for "hard work". Giving someone a bonus because they've been working so "hard" is nice, but that bonus may not have been necessary if the environment was a balanced and recoverable one.

You've got to be focused on your people, providing them with a great quality of life at work and at home. Yes, those companies do exist, and you can be one too! Place yourself in the shoes of your employees. Would you be attracted to your workplace? If you can't answer "yes" immediately, you need to look in the mirror and see the real problem. Time is precious. While everyone must work, you should not expect or require people to work as if your business owns them. You own the business, not the employees. Your employees are a privilege. People simply aren't going to continue working 6 and 7 days per week for someone else.

ACCEPTING TOXICITY

If the aforementioned areas are unacceptable, your workplace will become toxic. Many of the red flags below will start to pop up. You may not even realize it until you pull back for a full helicopter view. Here, I have laid out a comprehensive list that details 10 signs of a toxic workplace. It doesn't mean these are the only 10, however, these are usually the first 10 you see.

1. Management and ownership say, "Do whatever you have to do."
2. Dysfunctional HR department.
3. Removal of benefits, perks, and bonus programs.
4. Instilling fear and celebrating terminations.
5. Title obsession/that's not my job attitude.
6. Lack of empathy, guilt trips, angst, and anger.
7. Poorly run meetings.
8. Focusing on the bottom 10% and weaknesses.
9. Upper management vs ground-level management.
10. Lack of a friendly and welcoming atmosphere.

Let's go through the breakdown:

Toxic Sign #1: Management and ownership say, "Do whatever you have to do."

There's a big difference between upper management and ownership saying "Do whatever you think is right and feel is appropriate" vs. "Do whatever you have to do" or "Do whatever you need to do."

The first is a sign of trust and confidence in your employees' ability to make sound decisions. This is a positive thing. However, if you've ever told your people to do whatever they need to do, it's a clear sign that you either don't know a solution to the problem at hand, or simply do not care what your people need to do in order to achieve your goals. The problem could be HR issues or staffing issues. Most of the time, however, when employees are told to "do whatever you have to do" it's regarding financial performance of the business and a poorly written "pie in the sky" budget. With rare exceptions, greed creates nearly every single problem within a business. While "He who has the gold makes the rules", don't forget that "He who fails to follow the rules loses the gold."

Pushing people to hit ridiculous and unachievable budgets will set your business back years rather than inching it forward with proper growth. Reducing resources, negative prodding and cutting corners to hit a magnificently "written" bottom line absolutely destroys any business model. Telling your employees to do whatever they have to do is a clear sign your company has no idea of how to properly hit those pie-in-the-sky numbers. It's also a sign that the business owner isn't being honest with themselves about their own business. Are you *truly* underperforming or are you trying to break the bank overnight?

Counterproductive Culture

Don't create a problem just to say you have one. If you're not honest with yourself about the problem, you'll never address it properly. If problems aren't fixed properly, the business suffers, and so do all of your people. So, if you are telling your people to do whatever they need to do, make a change now. If not, you can guarantee that your employees understand you'll just keep pushing them until they burn out and they will leave for another venture before that happens.

Toxic Sign #2: A Dysfunctional HR department.

There are many ways in which a failing HR department will affect your workplace, and you should think of HR as the lifeline of good staffing. Employee attraction, hiring, and retention are all driven by a strong HR department. The first thing to look at is whether they are doing what they say they will do. In other words, are they meeting their goals?

When HR fails to meet admin goals, they're showing they do not have the desire or competence to fulfill the requirements. How can employees be expected to work hard and meet their numbers and metrics when the department that brought them in isn't meeting their own standards? A negative HR culture will trickle directly down to the employees and will rot your entire business. Similarly, if HR fails to return calls received from employees in a timely manner—or if they don't return them at all—they are failing at one of their most important obligations. HR is there to serve and protect the employees, just as the employees are there to serve and protect the company, and both must do their part. If there are constant issues with HR, there will be issues with the employees, too. One of these common issues occurs with payroll.

Frequent payroll issues can be absolutely heinous for employee trust and morale. Many times, issues are not corrected or take forever to correct. Payroll should be priority number one for all HR people. Your employees work for their checks. You want them to do anything they need do to for your business but do not want to ensure that their paycheck issues are taken care of immediately? Not taking immediate action to process correct payroll is a very bad sign that your HR reps are not concerned about positive culture and are unhappy with their jobs, too. When the HR department is unhappy, they will undoubtedly start to voice their negative opinions, which leads us to the next point.

When HR openly complains to employees about issues within the company, that is a clear sign of a dysfunctional HR department. It is HR's job to aid in producing and maintaining a stable and positive work environment, and if they themselves are openly dissatisfied and are sharing this with employees, your work culture is doomed. HR needs to be happy and satisfied with their work. This level of happiness will often manifest itself in how they keep their office and surroundings. An unorganized or dirty office tells you a lot. Keeping an unorganized office or an unclean office is a sign the HR reps do not take pride in their work and do not respect the people they are working for. And, perhaps, they do not respect themselves. This also shows a lack of standards and a lack of respect for all field-level management who are required to keep everything perfect. If your office has bowling ball sized holes in the walls, a dirty gummed-up carpet, filthy bathrooms, stained ceiling tiles, blown out light bulbs and dust everywhere, what makes you think people will look up to your HR reps and respect them? The answer is, they won't.

Another area that shows HR doesn't respect the people they serve is when they fail to stay on top of employee evaluation schedules and due dates. Many evaluations could be months, even years past due. This is a blatant disregard for the time and growth of the employees in the company. Staying on top of schedules, being prompt about duties and obligations, and even something as simple as dress code can show you how engaged and positive an HR department is. That's right, even something as simple as what they're wearing can tell you what is going on within your HR department.

Poor professional dress is a symbol of apathy at work. If employees can't be bothered to even stay in dress code, what makes you think they will perform their jobs well? While dress codes for office and field-level personnel may be different, they should both still be as reflective as possible to one another. If your field-level team is required to wear business professional dress, then your office staff should also be required to wear the same. If you see the office staff wearing ripped jeans and a designer shirt full of holes or personal slogans, they are setting a poor example for your field teams by not working to the same standard. You are also setting a poor example for your field teams by allowing your HR and other office departments to have a *lesser standard*. If you don't' keep the same standards, you won't be able to keep employees.

Showing Emotion. Do your HR reps become offended or upset when employees ask a question, challenge something, or bring a complaint to light? If so, this is a clear sign of an unapproachable and uncooperative HR department. Communication between employees and their HR reps should be open, free of negativity, and without emotion. If negativity and emotion do find their way into an HR department, ownership should address it immediately. When HR contributes to negativity and emotion, your people will have no one to turn to and no one to trust. An HR department full of emotion is one reflective of thinking that they are the boss, and they are the rule makers. This type of HR department has forgotten it's their job to enforce the local, state, and federal employment operating laws. This brings us to our next point.

You work for me. Another problem is when HR operates under an umbrella from ownership (personal needs and wants) rather than the umbrella of local, state, and federal authority. This is especially dangerous when HR is used as a tool in a discriminative way. They say with great power comes great responsibility, and I can think of no better adage to describe the responsibilities of an HR department. So, when HR is abused to serve personal business desires of ownership rather than protecting the business and its employees, the corruption that follows is unimaginable. Bettering the work lives of the employees they serve and doing right by them should be HR's only motivation.

Counterproductive Culture

As such, HR should listen thoroughly to employees. If your HR department does not listen and respond in a timely manner to issues and complaints brought forward from your employees, this will quickly lead to a feeling of dissatisfaction and further distrust. HR must respond appropriately. It is not sufficient to answer a question by telling someone to simply read the employee handbook or refer to a memo. Questions should be answered thoughtfully rather than advising employees to read from company policy statements in a closed, one-ended conversation. Employees should be allowed to voice their full concerns. They should not be shut down by an HR department that is acting as an angry or discriminatory arm for the business owner.

How's the weather today? Another interesting trick that dysfunctional HR reps use is changing subjects. When talking to employees who are expressing conflict, rather than addressing it with the employees involved, the subject gets changed into "proper training" or "scheduling" versus talking about the negative behaviors the employees have shown towards each other. Do not avoid a challenging issue by waffling around different topics instead of directly answering the posed question. Always address everything with the parties involved, right in front of one another, with multiple department heads on hand. Waffling is a form of fear. If your HR reps are afraid to have a direct conversation with your employees about any topic raised, it can be a sign of guilt and fear from the HR side. Guilt that they themselves did something wrong and need to now cover up for it or fear of the same. A waffling HR department is one of the most dangerous.

Policy last updated 4 years ago. Another problem is when the HR department rarely updates or asks for opinions from management on policies that may be outdated and require amending. If your company has policies in place that are backdated years ago with no updates, it is a sign of a disconnected HR department. Your HR department should ensure that policies are reviewed and updated monthly whenever applicable. If anything has changed and you expect your employees to be doing it, your policies need to reflect it. A proper handbook and training guides are key to having a successful environment with no gray areas. If your HR is failing to update your policies, they could be creating gray areas to protect themselves.

Toxic Sign #3: Removal of benefits, perks and bonus programs. Remember, it's not always about money. Your employees are looking for a total package to make their life work and provide you with their life's work. Is your company constantly changing health insurance plans and with each flip, the plan covers far less but costs employees far more? Health insurance is a right that employees deserve. When your health plans are hollow and don't offer much value, you're masquerading behind the promise of benefits when, in reality, you're barely offering anything at all.

Removing benefits that were a part of what attracted employees to the job such as 401k, life insurance, and additional long-term/short-term disability packages that were available is unacceptable to many employees. You should also beware of placing longer wait times for new employees before they are eligible to join health, 401k, and other benefits. Employees want the ability to make use of these benefits as quickly as possible. Creating your own delay makes your organization seem cheap and unreliable. It's a hard statement but, it's true. Perception is reality. Similarly, reducing the contributions you make to healthcare plans, 401k, and other available benefits, resulting in the employees having to pay more share while you try to save a couple of bucks is just as bad. Be generous to your employees, and they will be generous to you! Being stingy will only lead to dissatisfied workers down the line. Invest in the future—the future of your employees is the future of your company.

"Hands-on" Training. If you can't train, your employees can't explain. If they can't explain, then they can't perform. Removing training programs that were very valuable in keeping teams fresh and up to date is not an effective way of cost-cutting and saving labor. If these programs worked to improve your teams in the past, why not keep them around? Often, employers forget what made them successful in the past, and they unknowingly eliminate the positive programs that helped their company for years. Don't fall into this common yet unfortunate trap. The training period with your company is the most important period of any employee's tenure with you, especially during the first 100 days.

Recognition Counts. Perhaps the most vital thing employers do away with is recognizing employees for birthdays, surpassing goals, or some other award. Eliminating yearly celebrations or meetings where employees receive recognition and thanks for their accomplishments is ill-advised. Every chance to encourage and uplift an employee should be taken. The more positive the communication, the more motivated everyone gets. Make your employees feel valued and appreciated. If you eliminate forms of appreciation that offer positive communication, soon you'll only be communicating when problems occur. That creates a negative atmosphere. The more you communicate, the more positive things should become as problems are being solved. Any recognition program is a form of positive communication and should be a permanent part of your culture.

We're open late. Expanding business hours, resulting in employees working longer, including deciding to open on major holidays that the business has traditionally been closed for, is a good way to sabotage your culture. Changing your hours to have people work longer days feels like a bait and switch to your employees. They accepted employment and agreed on hours that were acceptable to them. But when those hours change, it's almost like reneging on a contract that was agreed upon. It's not what the employee agreed to, and it's not fair, especially when you do not compensate them for the extended hours of responsibility and work. Before you start expanding your hours, run a break-even formula to determine exactly how much money you will need to produce in top-line sales to pay for all the expanded investment hours. There will be more labor involved, utilities, product costs, etc. Will you be able to make more money on those expanded hours or are you only looking at the top-line without realizing you may end up losing money on the bottom-line due to it? While over-surveying your people is something you want to steer clear of, expanding business hours *is* something you should have your people opine on rather than forcing it down their throats. You may find that if you are compensating accordingly, you'll have plenty of team members who think it could be a great idea. Remember, everything is in the approach.

Raises are on hold. "The bottom line isn't at goal this year, we have to put all raises on hold." This is not something that should come as a surprise to anyone. If raises do need to go on pause due to business performance, it is something that should be communicated every single month with your people. Additionally, eliminating evaluations, extending evaluation periods for employees or eliminating raises altogether should obviously be avoided. This falls into the same "bait and switch" category. If conditions were that bad when the employees applied for the position, they probably wouldn't have accepted your employment in the first place. In the same vein, constantly changing the bonus program to "make it more financially appealing" when in actuality, the program gets harder to achieve with every change made, is equally as manipulative. Basically, many companies change their bonus program because they feel too many people are bonusing and they're paying too much out.

Cutting or changing bonus programs is a bad sign. Companies should *want* their employees to hit bonuses. If they're hitting a bonus, it means you as the employer are making the bottom line you budgeted! Taking away bonuses or making them impossible to reach only demotivates your employees. As such, employees will stop striving to hit and exceed their bottom line. In many cases, companies that change their bonus programs lose the employees altogether. The employer actually punishes an employee by removing bonuses when the bottom line is being hit. This is not an "inventive" way of growing your bottom line. It's the wrong message to send.

Mandatory 6th day. Adding mandatory hours to the permanent work schedule is just as unacceptable. Rather than having a 45-hour scheduled week, the company now states 50 hours is mandatory. Some even go from 50 to 55 hours. Some places even enact a mandatory 6th day so they can "hit their budgets" for certain periods of the year. This occurs frequently with employers who are located in snow zones. *"For*

Counterproductive Culture

the next 5 months, every salaried manager must work an 8-hour 6th day every week so we can pay our bills by saving labor."

Why would employees want to stay at your company when it keeps changing for the worse? Part of workplace stability is knowing things will not suddenly change. When places of work enact sweeping changes that are far from the norm they agreed upon accepting employment, it causes the environment to morph into a place of bitterness and negativity. If your workplace goes through multiple changes—they should be positive ones. Change is inevitable, but you cannot strip away all the positive aspects of the job that were the reason people applied in the first place. Why would they stay? Why would people give their time and lives to a company that takes from them more than it gives back? Invest in your people and they will go way above and beyond for you. Pinch your people and they will disappear quickly.

Toxic Sign #4: Fear and celebrating terminations.

Is your workplace full of fear? Are people constantly being threatened with their jobs? Are terminations celebrated? When fear has become a part of the daily work routine, your business is a sinking ship. Supervisors and leaders who employ this type of fear tactic as their form of motivation are actually sending a very clear message to their entire staff that they have no idea how to fix any problem and, have no idea how to manage people. When a leader gets to the point of threatening employees to get a response and results, it means they themselves have not role modeled what needed to be done, they have not worked on what needed to be worked and, they have lost the respect of their entire staff because of it.

This type of negative motivation creates a toxic work culture where everyone is walking on eggshells, and the anxiety of getting terminated creates a mental block for employees. Employee performance suffers, as they focus more on avoiding being fired rather than on their job duties. Which leads us to our next point.

If management believes motivating employees by threatening jobs and bullying is the best way to get more done, they are sorely mistaken. If phrases such as "or else" and "you'd better (do this)" are commonplace, you have a toxic and dangerous work environment that needs to be addressed. In this type of environment, team members fear for their position, even when they're performing as close to perfect as possible. Essentially, in creating this type of fearful atmosphere, you've rendered everyone ineffective. This is a counterproductive culture. No one should have to carry around this type of anxiety and stress while they attempt to do their jobs. An angry manager is a manager who has failed to do their part of the work. An angry owner is an owner who has failed to choose the right people for his team and has failed to set realistic goals for them. Do you really think that bullying people and threatening them with their jobs will make them perform better? It won't. What it will do, however, is create a team full of enemies who will drop a slew of HR and other legal complaints into your lap as they try to protect themselves.

Counterproductive Culture

Forms redacted. "We won't tell you what your financial performance was, but we will tell you it was bad, and you need to work harder!" Your workplace is in jeopardy when communication about business performance is not readily available or is hidden from employees. This often occurs when profit and loss statements are only provided showing certain line items rather than releasing the entire thing. How are goals and metrics to be met when performance information is not fully available? Is management even giving employees a chance to meet their goals? Are the goals being met but not shared? When employees ask questions about business performance, are they shut down and told to mind their own business? Unclear metrics, or the unwillingness to talk about them, is a clear sign of a dysfunctional workplace. It makes your people uneasy and leaves them with a desire to join a group that offers improved transparency.

He said, she said. Another sign of a crumbling work culture is whispering and gossiping. Many times, the gossip is about management coming down on employees and displaying negative behaviors. It starts to pass around with everyone and soon, all of your employees have heard about your angry behavior. This results in immediate loss of respect from your people. This kind of tension at a workplace is stifling, and it suffocates employees' moods and productivity. It is only natural for people to speak to one another about their experiences in your company. If you provide poor ones, they will make their way around to everyone.

Blanket management. It gets even worse when those whispers come to life in the form of emails. Many times, mass emails are sent where everyone is punished or threatened due to the actions of one. I refer to this as *blanket management.* This is when leaders do not take the time to speak individually with everyone but rather take a shortcut and "blanket" the entire staff with the issue, even when the rest of the staff has not partaken in any wrongdoing. This creates a landslide of whispering and gossip. Blanket management does the exact opposite of the short-sighted intended goal. If you have something to discuss where your entire employee base needs to be blanketed, create the updated policy and review it live with everyone, face to face. This way you can answer questions and provide proper reasoning behind the move versus just email blasting policies in a cold fashion.

Teachers pet. Another concerning trend is when people fight in management's favor because they feel if they're a "favorite" they'll have a better chance at keeping their position or even gaining promotion. If an employee feels they must succumb to this type of brownnosing, your work culture has turned into an everybody for themselves survival mission. This usually develops when others within your group have been promoted or been given special treatment over those who have outperformed them. This obliterates teamwork and communication, because instead of working together and matching each other's effort, employees will work selfishly and independently.

Counterproductive Culture

Similarly, when employees constantly feel that nothing they do is good enough to satisfy upper management and ownership, this shows a culture of negativity and dissatisfaction. Employees and management should feel encouraged by their achievements, not scared and skeptical that nothing they do will be appreciated

Internal conflict. "I don't care what the other manager just told you. They were wrong and this is what I want done!" Management complaining about other management or even ownership is also a terrible sign. Ideally, no one in a company or business should be speaking negatively about anyone. I recall consulting for a very large employer, where the owner was constantly beating his chest that his people were happy. As I introduced myself to everyone, I found quite the opposite to be true. Internal conflict was everywhere. Not one department within this group was happy with their roles. HR, Finance, Maintenance, Operations, Executives, none of them spoke positively. In fact, out of over 12,000 employees, I could not find one person who didn't complain about the company. Everyone was extremely angry and bitter. Even the Vice President was audibly dissatisfied and cited corruption at the highest rank! If you're at odds with each other, success is simply impossible. The number of conflicts coming from the organization will distract employees from their duties and overwhelm them. How can they focus on the challenges of their roles when they must deal with difficulties amongst their own staff? An entire organization must work together as a cohesive team to be successful, and squabbles among them will only detract from their momentum. When you hear management voicing their displeasure about other leaders within your company, it's a clear sign of a broken group with poor management.

I fired them today! "We would like to announce that as of today, we have terminated your General Manager for poor performance!" Have you ever heard someone telling a story about another person being fired? Often, this is something companies try to celebrate, laughing and joking as if it's commonplace and entertaining. I've actually witnessed an employer parallel multiple employee firings they performed in a 24-hour period to the Night of the Long Knives, championing it as if they just took their company back. (The Night of the Long Knives was a turning point in German history where within the German government, Hitler was established as the Supreme Administrator of Justice for all the German people.)[1] Other times, I've seen employers make light of terminations, picturing and portraying themselves as a makeshift mafia, such as the Corleone's from The Godfather in saying "Today, we settled all family business." It's disgusting and disturbing. If stories about terminating employees are frequently shared as happy anecdotes, fun conversations or stories trying to instill power, your work environment has eroded. This is the point at which a company's revolving door is wide open. Celebrating a termination in any shape or form is a tactic done by weak management and weak ownership. Pay

---

[1] Shirer, William L. *The Rise and Fall of the Third Reich: A History of Nazi Germany*. New York: Simon & Schuster, 1960.

close attention to this; it is especially important, as it is never positive to terminate anyone. In terminating someone, you're damaging that person's life as well as that of their family, regardless of what they may have done. Talking about terminating an employee, especially smearing them in any way, should never be done. Doing this sends a message to employees who will wonder what will be said or has been said about them.

Toxic Sign #5: Title obsession/that's not my job attitude.
"That's not my job", "I don't get paid for that", "That's not in my job description." Do you hear management and employees alike say things like this? This can happen on every level of the totem pole from the top to the bottom. If you hear anything like this in your work environment, it immediately tells you employees feel overworked and underappreciated. It also tells you executive management is not on par with what positive and consistent leadership should be. Those employees who are complaining have probably gone way above and beyond for their employer on multiple occasions and were not rewarded for it as they were told they would be.

In addition, this can also be a sign of favoritism and failure by management to hold everyone to the same standards. Frequently, employees who voice their pushback on job duties in this fashion are the ones who have accomplished the most. However, they saw little to no reward while others who underperformed and underachieved received the same pay, bonus, and rewards. They are voicing opinions as others were allowed to be ineffective while they were pushed very hard to do more. When people aren't rewarded as they were told, this is called "dangling the carrot". Oftentimes, employers will motivate you to put extra work in by promising you a greater reward. But, when the work is done, that carrot gets pulled back until you achieve another goal. This keeps repeating itself without end and the employee who puts in all of the extra work gets nothing or only gets a small fraction of what they were originally promised. Dangling the carrot is a very quick way to create a negative, title-obsessed, "that's not my job" attitude within your entire company. It only takes one time for someone to learn you're fooling them with false promises. Once they learn it, you'll never get the same level of effort again.

Prior precedent. Many times, employees who should be disciplined for certain things aren't but employees who make a simple mistake while trying their absolute best are. Failing to hold everyone to the same standard is a sign of weak management. It is also a huge sign that management is afraid to step up to the plate should they turn someone over. This type of leader wants to be hands-off and allows anyone to get away with anything so they can keep their own helicopter view. At the same time, leaders like this will keep riding the "thoroughbreds" to "deal" with ongoing people issues all while doing nothing to assist or resolve them. Anything will be done to keep their hands off and prevent themselves from having to work harder. Failing to follow the same progressive discipline precedents with every employee is also a

Counterproductive Culture

sign of favoritism. A mistake is a mistake, and a problem is a problem. It should not matter who made the mistake or created the problem. All that should matter is that the exact same company policies are followed, in order, for every single employee. The prior precedents you have previously set for the same actions should be what is done at every occurrence, regardless of the person. Anything less will create anger and distrust amongst the rest of your teams. It will also open you up to legal battles.

Match each other's effort. Not everyone has the same skillset and abilities, but everyone should be matching each other's efforts to achieve goals. That's right, what everyone can do to be successful as a team is to *match each other's efforts*! If management does nothing but push the highest performing, best-skilled team members without focusing equally on less skilled but still valuable team members who need development and training to succeed, that environment will always struggle. No one can accomplish as much individually as an entire team can. Focus on what all members of the team *can* do and utilize their strengths to help your other team members focus on things that no one else is able to do. If everyone on the team does their best to match each other's efforts in accomplishing their skillset goals, you'll see a wholehearted change in your group. Your top performers will be appreciative of everyone helping them achieve new heights and your mid-level performers will feel great that they were part of a team that helped get there where they too were rewarded. Not everyone can be a star quarterback. However, everyone can be a star of the team where the quarterback led them to victory.

Toxic Sign #6: Lack of empathy, guilt trips, angst, and anger.
Is your workplace's leadership frequently blinded by emotion? Do they lose the ability to take a different approach based on individual personality? Making decisions based on emotion is unwise and ineffective. Being set in your ways will make it difficult to train and relate to everyone. Your employees are signing up for a dynamic and positive workplace. They aren't signing up to be in the military. There isn't a one-size-fits-all method for how to manage everyone. Your team is comprised of individuals who may all learn in different ways. If you're not flexible enough to meet people where they are and adjust, you'll never be a successful leader. Everyone may have different things that will motivate them to get the work done well. Some people want extra praise, some people want extra communication, some people want autonomy, some people want to be micromanaged, some people want high-level energy, some people want to talk about their family all the time and some people don't want to talk about anything other than work and just getting the job done. It is up to you to learn the personalities of your people and turn the keys appropriately to help open the doors of success with them.

Counterproductive Culture

Oh, woe to me! Speaking of turning the keys, a particularly disturbing tactic in toxic management is when leadership will openly discuss their own personal cash flow issues with their employees. This is often done in an attempt to gain sympathy with the hopeful result that employees will work more hours and "catch up" on things to help improve the bottom line or even, "fill in" for them so they can tend to their personal matters.

Purposefully mentioning your personal struggles as leverage to make an employee work harder is simply not acceptable. The lack of honesty and integrity in such a strategy is evident. It leaves no room on your team or in your workplace for openness, appreciation, and fairness. You certainly wouldn't want to be managed in this fashion so, why do it to those who work for you? Save the drama. Just tell your people what is really going on and ask them to do what you need. They will appreciate it far more than the "woe to me" approach.

I need to see your doctor's note. Another problem that is equally unfair and inappropriate is when an employee must use some sick time but receives treatment as if they're lying about it. When an employee calls in sick, it's followed by a slew of calls from management asking questions about their health. "How long do you think you'll be out?" "When are you coming back?" "You can't be out that long, you have responsibilities." "I've had the same thing before, and it doesn't take that long to recover."

The interrogation is then almost always followed by trying to get hard dates when they'll be back, even when the employee has already provided that info via doctor's note.

After the initial conversation, many company leaders still continue to call employees daily while they're on sick leave rather than respecting their privacy and letting them rest. *This is one of the absolute worst things an employer can do.* You've got to understand, when an employee is out, they're out. There's nothing that can get them back sooner other than healing. The more stress you put on an employee to come back quicker, the longer it will end up taking. The stress you add to your employee when you do this slows their healing process and causes more damage than you think. Aside from that, when you do this, you lose all respect you've gained with your employee up to this point. They work hard for you. You get sick and call them for support to cover you. So, why don't you give them the proper support they need when they're ill, too?

We need to cancel your vacation. Have you ever made an employee feel guilty about taking their well-earned vacation time? With many leaders, when an employee tries to take vacation, they are met with calls focused on the "urgency of the workplace" as if it will fall apart while they're out. Often, employees are asked to change the vacation, take less days or break it up into a few days off at a time. There is an old trick here of convincing employees to take "a few long weekends" rather than taking the time they deserve. This is a way supervisors lower their own workload by ensuring they don't have to report to field levels and physically work them while employees are out.

    Furthermore, there are also times when, on specific days, management or ownership will ask employees to meet them at the office, or even their own home, to discuss "business" and talk about how to "improve". Employees are made to feel like they're an owner in many conversations. In reality, most employees have no ownership stake. "Ownership mentality" applies here. Employers fail to realize that taking employees away from their families on their day off is not the best approach in motivating people to do more. It's not the best way to bend your employees' ear and get them to "work harder" or have an "ownership mentality". If you want your people to have an "ownership mentality" where they will cancel vacations and work without schedules, give them a true ownership stake in the business, even if it is a miniscule one. This doesn't mean a bonus program either. If you expect your people to be available 24/7 then you should reward them accordingly for running your business and actually make a small part of it theirs while they are employed with you. There are plenty of companies out there that provide an immediate percentage of bottom-line profits back to their lead team members for these exact reasons. This is on top of any bonus program that is in place. No one can truly understand and have an ownership mentality unless they are owners and, no one will have that ownership mentality should you keep taking their personal time away.

No empathy for you! How about when leadership wants empathy from their employees even when they themselves are never empathetic? Oftentimes, leaders expect empathy from employees when discussing their own personal and financial issues but, should employees have personal or financial issues they're trying to discuss professionally, they are met with anger, angst, and are oftentimes made to feel like they're an inconvenience. This kind of hypocrisy will kill any positive work culture you have. If you can help make things easier for an employee to be successful with you by offering some type of support, do it! If you can't, be honest about it, however, be sure to show respect in that process and give them the time they deserve when speaking with you.

"I just bought a lake house and two Mercedes-Benz."
"Oh, and I forgot to mention that my wife spent $40,000 on draperies for the lake house, too. So, raise prices and cut labor because I've just spent a lot of my own personal money."

Yes, I've actually worked with people who have announced these exact things to their employees in an effort to make them work harder and gain empathy for their own personal spending issues. A half-million-dollar lake house, two new Mercedes and a new Jeep for the three children who just turned driving age. A new Mercedes for the wife as well as one for himself. And yes, $40,000 spent on draperies. There are a million more of these outrageous examples that I can share just like this. All of them followed by telling their people that times are tough, and everyone needs to work harder! It would seem with this type of personal spending that times are great and you're reaping the benefits of them. Why make times tough for your people when it's not needed?

Leaders need to be mindful and considerate of their employees and their financial situations. While you are not responsible for the personal spending habits of your employees, you are responsible for how you choose to share yours. If you can personally burn through one million dollars in a month, then you'd better not tell your employees you aren't able to provide them with a standard cost of living pay raise or that you must remove their bonuses as the company isn't performing well. If you're spending money, it's very obvious your company is doing great, and your employees should be doing equally as great.

Francesco R. Benzo

"Little Silvio - Hard Times"

Counterproductive Culture

If management and ownership openly speak about things they buy, own, or the money they have spent, this can be very dangerous. You need to be mindful of your people because while you're flaunting your success, your team may be struggling just to make ends meet with food on the table.

Don't forget, your success has partially been provided to you by your employees and their hard work. What money would you be making without them? Flaunting your successes can be a big slap in the face to the people who work for you. Especially with companies that have denied raises and have decreased benefits. Your people will dislike you for this type of behavior. They will leave you and you'll end up doing the one thing you no longer want to do, *work hard.* Stay away from this type of behavior. Stay humble and appreciative. Do you remember when you were a child and tried to bring bubble gum into class? You were probably told, "If you don't have enough bubble gum for everyone, don't bring it to class." Flaunting your wealth with your employees is the same thing. If you aren't going to spread and share the wealth, don't flaunt yours.

Toxic Sign #7: Poorly run meetings.

Meetings are an essential method of communication and moral building in the workplace, but if any of the following is happening with your meetings, it may be time to examine your company culture.

I'll be there in 5 minutes. Are people frequently late for meetings or skip them entirely? If employees don't take meetings seriously, it's highly doubtful they take their jobs seriously, either. If they're showing up late or missing meetings for another reason, it's important to figure out why. Perhaps they don't feel like a true part of the team? Whatever the case, your employees need to be active participants in your meetings. But these meetings also need to be scheduled intelligently and conscientiously.

If meetings are scheduled on employees' days off, you're creating a problem. Employees need to be put in a position where they can be present for any meeting. If not, how can you blame them for being unable to show up? You certainly can't keep expecting them to attend meetings on their day off. Your employees will pick up quickly that you're trying to save payroll and get them for extra "free time" rather than pay them to be at your office on normal schedule. Your employees understand this mandatory meeting on a day off is typically done where salaried managers do not get paid for attending a now 6th or 7th day of work. Employees get pulled in on their day off with no regard to their quality of life. This is a particularly bad sign should this be happening in your workplace.

It's also an issue if members of management and ownership fail to attend the meetings at all. This goes for when they're late attending scheduled appointments and sit-downs with employees as well. Again, management needs to be held to the same standard as the employees who work for them. When this isn't the case, the inconsistency will leave a bitter taste in your team's mouth.

It is just as bad if meetings are cut short because management does not want to spend the amount of time originally scheduled as they have "other things to do". Staff may also be informed their time is "better spent" going back to work versus sharing vital information that can help them succeed with the full meeting.

The best practice is to keep meetings scheduled on a frequency and on a calendar where everyone has access to view them. If meetings are scheduled at the last minute, many times it's an emotional response to something rather than a standard communication that helps keep everyone on track. Meetings are a useful tool to communicate with and inspire your teams, but they can only be beneficial if they're used properly and purposefully. Use meetings in a way that enhances your company and teams. Don't make them something that everyone dreads. Employees looking forward to meetings might be the single biggest indicator that you are using meetings correctly and everyone wants to be involved.

Toxic Sign #8: Focusing on the bottom 10% and weaknesses.
Focusing on the bottom 10% is a practice that was originally introduced by former GE CEO, Jack Welch. It refers to focusing on your lowest level performers to either improve or remove them from your organization. This is a good practice when done with care and proper efforts. However, many groups take this practice to an entirely new level. To what extent is your company investing money and time into your stated lowest performing people? Are you truly trying to help them learn and improve or if they don't perform immediately are you just trying to get them out?

Does your company spend as much time praising and rewarding the top 90% as it does focusing on the bottom 10%? If not, you've got a toxic, angry culture focused only on negativity and mistakes.

A mistake made in good judgement. Everyone will make mistakes. Not even a robot is perfect all of the time. As a leader, you must realize and recognize if those mistakes were made with good judgement or in poor judgement.

If someone makes a mistake in good judgement, it means they tried to resolve a problem using their best efforts. This type of mistake should be acceptable and used as a positive learning opportunity. Afterall, you *want* your people taking action and trying to resolve issues as they occur. If the mistake is made in poor judgement, you should understand the actions were purposefully detrimental and really were not a mistake at all. When looking at the bottom 10%, it's these individuals whom you should be focusing your efforts on.

However, if leadership is just insanely focused on turning anyone over who makes a mistake, you have a problem. With this, oftentimes leadership will also focus on turning over anyone who aggravates or challenges them, even if they are a high performer. As always, the focus should be on the positive and not the negative. Who wants to spend their days working at a place that focuses mostly on their shortcomings? Life is challenging enough without having your mistakes constantly highlighted and emphasized. Before you challenge someone on their mistakes, look at your own past experiences and see how people have handled yours. If you felt positive about how someone handled a mistake you made, then adopt that method when speaking with your people. If you didn't enjoy or respond to the way someone handled a mistake with you, then you shouldn't pass that negativity on. Find a new way to reach your people and help them learn. Don't forget, mistakes are often the best learning tool anyone can have.

You did this 5 years ago. Another related problem is when past mistakes are held over everyone's head no matter how long ago the initial issue was. Leadership brings up those past mistakes, even when they're not relative to the conversation at hand and no matter how long ago they were. Past errors are also brought up without recourse for hard how someone has worked to correct them. Torturing employees with old mistakes is unproductive and simply wrong. Mistakes are opportunities for growth, and they should be treated that way, which leads to the next point.

You're on my list. Management will sometimes create lists of people they need to focus on turning over versus lists of people that should be trained and promoted! Once again, this focus on the negative instead of the positive—on turning over rather than developing—is highly detrimental. It is demotivating and toxic.

Employees in this type of environment will not feel motivated to achieve goals by doing more but rather they will feel uncomfortably pushed and pressured to do so. There will always be a list of things that need to be improved but, do you leverage and recognize the things that are going well to help build morale and focus that positive energy onto completing the next tasks, or do you only focus on the negatives? At some point, that negativity will burn your people out completely.

You've lost your bonus. Even more despicable is when leadership removes raises or bonuses from employees due to a mistake they've made. Rather than taking the employees' entire 6 month or 1-year period of work into consideration, greedy leaders choose to remove the bonuses or raises at the first opportunity they see, even when someone has been a great performer.

Counterproductive Culture

It really isn't fair to make such a decision based on one or two slip ups when an employee has given you months, or even years of solid work. Evaluate someone as a whole, not just by one of their parts. We all have fallen short and missed the mark, and we all will again in the future. Do not punish someone for simply being *human*. Taking away something they have earned will result in your people becoming quiet quitters. They will show up, however, will do nothing but the bare minimum to get by and at some point, they will quit altogether.

We need everyone's attention. When someone does make a mistake, it's important not to take it out of context. One person making a mistake doesn't mean that everyone on your team needs to be retrained or that new policies need to be implemented. It means one person needs to be retained and coached on the error so they can learn and move forward. It really is that simple.

Don't judge and punish your entire team based on a small handful of people. You should not blanket all your employees with new policies due to the actions of a few. And your company should not change celebratory meetings and events only to turn them into mandatory "come to Jesus" meetings. Focus on your employees' growth and try not to focus so much on shortcomings. The more you recognize the positives in your employees, the easier it is to speak with them about the mistakes.

Francesco R. Benzo

This is the worst President in American history! There are other things besides focusing on mistakes that can take too much of your bandwidth as a leader. Dwelling too much on anything other than your teams' growth will be very harmful to your entire organization. News and politics seem to be the most energy-sucking focuses with many companies over the last 16 years. This is extremely unadvisable. Neither you nor your employees have any control over outside distractions, especially with politics. Harping about them all day will

wear on your employees very quickly. They will get sick of it and sick of you. Especially if their political opinions don't match up with yours.

Your workplace should only be focused on what it can control within its own walls. Any other focus is counterproductive. Stop complaining about the world around you and create your own positive world within your company for yourself and your employees.

Counterproductive Culture

"Little Silvio - Controlling Your Four Walls"

Toxic Sign #9: Management vs Management vs Employees.

Is your executive-level management a separate group that rarely interacts with ground-level management? I sure hope not. If any of the following points apply to your management climate, it's time for some huge change.

It's usually one-way communication. Do your executives make decisions with zero collaboration from anyone else, especially during meetings. If different members of your team aren't allowed and encouraged to participate in open communication, your workplace is broken. Communication needs to flow both ways, and not just from leadership to employees. If something is changing, every single employee should be allowed to opine prior.

It doesn't matter what you think. We want your opinion…not really. When opinions and ideas are asked for, are they usually bounced back quickly to your people with an unthoughtful response that immediately disagrees? Are your people made to feel as if in giving their opinion they're the problem or are creating an issue? I hope this is not the case. This kind of deflection is rude and patronizing. It will not only result in employees avoiding sharing their ideas in the future, but it will also increase turnover very quickly. If you truly aren't interested in hearing opinions, then stop asking for them. Based on the way you respond, your people will learn quickly if you're just asking for opinions to say, "we do it, too" and pretend you have a great culture. This leads us to our next point.

We need your response in 24 hours or less. Many times, companies will solicit employees for feedback and give a deadline as to when said feedback should be received. This is frequently done with surveys. Employees are pushed to and sometimes mandated to provide feedback, with a short deadline as to when they can. First off, putting a short deadline on enabling employees to provide feedback is a huge mistake. Yes, there should always be a closing date for a survey, however, if it's too short then you're over-pressuring your employees to provide you with feedback! If you're going to run surveys, keep them open for 30 days. This way your employees can have proper time to think about and professionally articulate the things they wish to inform you of. When that feedback is given during a 30-day window, you should provide a weekly update to your teams as to how the survey feedback is stacking up! Too many times companies pressure their employees for quick feedback but take forever to provide the information back to their people, if at all! In soliciting information from your teams, you should provide information back within the same amount of time you expected to receive it. Should you fail to, your feedback will continue to get worse and many of your employees may not do your surveys at all.

Send me an email. "Just reach out to me with an email, I'll get back to you." How many times do you say that? Do you, as a leader, deflect things and tell employees to just put what they need in an email? How long do those emails take before you reply to them? How many times have you not replied to them at all? The same can be said for phone calls. If issues brought up the chain are usually ignored, it's a sign that management can't be bothered to assist and respond to employees as needed. This will result in your employees making a choice to stop communicating with you and just stick to their own routine. If you ignore them, they will ignore you. At this point, when communication finally does occur, it's too late and often results in a hard conversation, which is our next point.

You'd better do this or else. When leadership communicates with employees, they should be kind and helpful, not frustrated or threatening. It should be free of emotion and never "short on time". Too many times, employees are spoken to with negative emotion, short conversations that do not allow for full context of actual events and poor motivational tactics that threaten. Typical verbiage used in these situations are, "You'd better do this", "if you don't", and "or else". All of these allude to termination of the employee. These are poor choices of communicative style. If you're going to terminate someone, just tell them what they're doing wrong, and should it continue, it will result in termination. There is no need to fearmonger in trying to get your employee to perform for you. If you need to manage using this type of fear tactic, you've either hired the wrong employee or you've turned the employee completely off with your poor management style.

Dropping a bomb. Speaking of fearmongering, leaders also should not attempt to show off or intimidate, especially using swear words. This is not a good sign. It is a fear tactic when management feels it motivating to "pump everyone up" by dropping swear words during team meetings or even in one-on-one conversations. Attempting to instill fear in this fashion isn't a motivator to your employees. It's a rotten tactic that weak leaders use in trying to show everyone they are "the boss." The leader who does this is actually the weakest one in the entire group. This also brings up a double standard. You would fire your employees for swearing in the workplace and certainly for swearing at you. Why is it ok for you to swear at them in the workplace? It isn't. Clean your mouth out and start treating people with respect.

I'll take the credit. Speaking of respect, another issue that troubles your workers is when goals met and achieved are not recognized. Many times, credit and recognition for the accomplishments will be taken by executives when they've not even contributed one thing to the project. If you're getting credit for the hard work of your staff, you need to give them credit, too. Not just one-on-one but publicly, to your entire organization. Everything is a team effort and there's not one set of hands on this earth that can do more than many sets of hands working together. Raise your employees' hands as yours are being raised and allow them to join you in some limelight.

Toxic Sign #10. Unfriendly atmosphere.

Do you notice people tend not to greet each other? Things as simple as saying "hello" or "goodbye" are nonexistent? If friendliness and common courtesy are absent at your place of business, that says a lot about leadership and company culture. Imagine spending most of your day at a place that is cold and unwelcoming. Considering most people spend more time at work than they do with their families, interactions at the office should be friendly and positive. Smiles should not be hard to find and people in general should be happy working for you. Just as things should be friendly while employees are at work, they should come in with just as much positivity.

When employees arrive for shifts in a sour mood, it's obvious they don't want to be there—and you need to ask yourself why. Supervisors play a vital role in setting the tone for the workplace environment. When supervisors rarely ask how anyone is doing, it tells the employees that their well-being is not a significant concern. All they care about is that the employee comes in to get their work done. That is a very 1970s and 1980s style of cold and demanding management that has long been unfavorable with any workforce.

Counterproductive Culture

When this type of impersonal culture is in place, the employees may treat each other in the same manner.

Another sign of indifference, or even bitterness, is when employees tend to not look at each other while speaking. This kind of robotic and impersonal atmosphere can be a sign that employees have mentally "checked out". This often occurs when management does nothing but berate employees with every breath. Blah blah blah! All they do is complain, belittle and yell! No one likes people who do this and no one wants to work with someone they don't like, let alone have to look at them while being scolded. Berating is a quick way to make your people stop liking you.

You see, even in answering the phone, supervisors may inhibit positive culture. Having a rushed tone saying things like "What's up", "What do you want?" or "Yep" are all curt answers that make it clear to your employees you don't want to be bothered.

Don't laugh. Are laughing and general conversations discouraged in your workplace? Do you constantly tell your people to "quiet down" or even, to stop talking all-together? This too is a very 1970s and 1980s style of management. This type of atmosphere reduces the employees' work life down to sneaking around and walking on eggshells. They are afraid to speak up, have a laugh, or otherwise enjoy themselves. If you're running a sweatshop then say so. Otherwise, people were given voices for a reason and it's ok for your employees to have an occasional laugh or two. Laughing is the best medicine. If you discourage it, you're poisoning your workplace.

Where did they go? Do employees fail to report to their supervisor before leaving their shift? No one knows where they went, they just leave. If employees avoid leadership so much that even when they're about to leave for the day, they'd rather not interact with them, it's a clear sign of the indifference in your workplace. A leader cannot be successful if the people they lead want nothing to do with them!

Ultimately, if you have noticed any—or several—of these ten signs, your work environment may be starting to boil. Remember, though, as an employer it's not enough to be on the lookout for a negative workplace atmosphere. It's also your responsibility to contribute positively to the environment. Perhaps the simplest way to do this is to be kind and polite.

Have you ever asked someone how they're doing, and they say "Good" but don't ask you anything polite in return? Manners still count. Dave Thomas, successful businessman and founder of Wendy's, highlights this in his book, *Dave's Way*. Dave lived by the Golden Rule: Treat others the way you want to be treated. He simplified this by saying, Just Be Nice. Respect is how you treat everyone, not just in how you treat people you're trying to impress or believe you need in order to succeed. You should always treat everyone with respect, even if you don't know who they are. It's amazing that some companies still treat people poorly. It's disappointing that those leaders creating the culture cannot be thankful for where they are and thankful to the

Counterproductive Culture

people who are willing to help them by being employees. Perhaps everyone needs a reminder to "just be nice."

2
THE FIRST PROBLEM YOU SEE IS NOT THE ROOT CAUSE OF THE PROBLEM

In the dawn of high-rise buildings, New York building owners faced an interesting problem. Elevators took too long, and people hated them. People said they were simply too slow. Different companies and specialists were brought in to remediate the problem.

The first would-be solution was to make them faster. Simple, right? The elevators are too slow, so speed them up! Turns out, making them faster only made people dizzy and sick to their stomachs. Handsome sums of money were spent to speed up the elevators, but when that didn't make people happy, the building owners were at a loss for what could be done. Then a young man came along and proposed a different solution. Interestingly, he focused on psychology rather than elevator performance.

"The elevators aren't too slow," he stated. "The people are bored." He then formulated a plan to install mirrors in the elevators to give people something to look at. He also implemented visual floor indicators so they could judge how much time was left until they made it to their floor. His plans were put in motion and were wildly successful. These new ideas cost half as much as the previous ideas. It turns out the elevators weren't too slow, after all.

Counterproductive Culture

Problem-solving in the workplace is a necessity. As different personalities, management styles, and opinions converge, there will inevitably be conflicts and issues that arise. Having a good foundation from which to solve these problems and build back team morale is vital for the health and growth of your team. Perhaps the first thing one should do is to take a step back and realize there may be more going on than you think. In short, the first issue you see—or think you see—may not be telling the entire story. The first problem you see is often not the root cause of the problem.

What you see first could likely be a manifestation of a different issue, the culmination of a longstanding conflict, or a combination of these. To make sure you're seeing things clearly, don't make one single assumption. Individually ask, listen, and document what the people working for you have to say. Don't take what you've been told by others as the complete truth. You may find those truth-tellers you're listening to are protective-motivated in hiding their own flaws and are hiding what is really happening from you.

Protective motivation theory deals with how people evaluate threats and handle stressful situations. The theory suggests that people protect themselves in two ways: assessing the situation by determining its severity and deciding how to respond to the situation—or how to cope. These are called threat appraisal and coping appraisal. In the case of a protective-motivated employee hiding the truth from you, they have determined that the threat is very serious, and the best way to cope is to make sure you don't find out the truth. Don't forget, the person who wants you to trust them the most is usually the one you should trust the least.

It is also paramount to be flexible with your viewpoints. Always be willing to consider different points of view, and don't look at someone with a difference of opinion as disagreeing with you. They simply have a different opinion from their perspective. Everyone's perception is their reality, and their reality is a part of your company.

If you only associate with people who believe the same things as you do, how will you ever learn anything new? Being surrounded by colleagues with the same views and ideas as yourself is called being in an "echo chamber", where all sentiments, viewpoints, and thought processes are mirrored and shared. This is not conducive to growth, and old ways of doing business are unlikely to ever be challenged or improved.

Echo chambers stifle creativity and innovation. While it may be soothing to the ego, never being told that you're wrong and having everyone always agree with you does nothing to improve yourself or your company. You want people with intellectual curiosity who question and challenge things and aren't afraid to ask "why". This is especially crucial for your leaders.

When choosing leaders, it is very important to seek out those who *will* provide you with a *different point of view*. As a leader, you must be able to draw out what both sides of the coin can look like. This can only be done by surrounding yourself with all perspectives.

With this, it's extremely important to alternate the team leads within your committees and ancillary groups multiple times per year. If

Counterproductive Culture

you keep the same people as leaders all year, you'll only be focusing on the items those leaders feel are important and their personal opinions will become the main focus of those groups. Those focus areas and opinions are valid, however, if you don't rotate your team leaders, you're failing to diversify your focus areas, opinions, and points of view. This means you're failing to explore possibilities and opportunities within your company to make improvements.

Listen to people with different opinions and points of view. Put those people on your teams as leads, in rotation. You'll find the entire agenda changes and there are far more opportunities to improve than you realized.

SWEEP IT UNDER THE RUG!

We've all heard the expression "Don't sweep things under the rug". This becomes especially important in the workplace. One of the most common boons of ineffective problem-solving are quick fixes that end up sweeping the real issues under the rug.

There truly is no such thing as a quick fix. All you're doing is temporarily masking the problem until it rears its ugly head down the road. You're just stowing problems away to deal with later.

One common area where this often happens is avoiding necessary repairs. A company may not want to spend the time or money repairing broken or malfunctioning equipment—but those fixes must be made, and there's really no way around it. By sweeping such repairs under the rug, you're essentially waiting on a ticking time bomb. The neglected equipment will only get worse over time, most likely leading to more expensive repairs down the line. Why wait to fix something later when you can do it now? Especially when waiting means things will likely get worse and there will be an even bigger mess to clean up. Don't sweep necessary repairs under the rug—you are only creating a bigger problem for yourself and for your people.

Counterproductive Culture

"Little Silvio – Problem Solving"

Another unfortunate area employers fall short while problem solving is putting off employee evaluations. It is essential for employees to know where they stand—to understand what they are doing well versus the things they may need to work on. Delaying, or even, completely avoiding employee evaluations is a serious disservice to your workers and your business. The longer you go without meeting with your employees to discuss their progress, the longer bad habits and complacency will be allowed to marinade. In fact, failing to evaluate your employees as per your company policy will also lead to an increase in employee dissatisfaction, lower work performance and increased turnover rates.

What's more, the employee is left in the dark, unsure of what they bring to your company and unsure of how to improve. Don't sweep employee evaluations under the rug. They should be done promptly and thoroughly. There is no better way to ensure the efficiency and success of your company than making sure your employees have what they need to succeed. Would you not be upset if your personal evaluation wasn't done by your employer? Yes, you would. Your employees feel the same way when you fail to do theirs. It's also important for your employees to have a voice. Sitting down with them during their evaluations is a good time for them to let you know anything that might be bothering them or getting in the way of their success.

The same thing can be said about paying bills. Many employers will ignore or brush off bills—either waiting until more profits are earned to pay them or simply putting them off until later.

Counterproductive Culture

This mentality is dangerous. The bills need to be paid regardless of the amount of profit you bring in, so why delay when you're able to pay it? Businesses will always have overhead; electricity bills will always need to be paid; suppliers will always require payment for their products and services. Waiting to pay these bills is just frustrating for everyone. Better to take care of them right away than to let them accumulate. This is also a quick way to lose a great vendor. They performed a service for you and expect to be paid. That vendor may be counting on your payment to take care of their family. Don't forget that.

Another thing you cannot afford to sweep under the rug is bad behavior. When you let bad behavior slide without addressing it, you are reinforcing these actions and telling whoever is exhibiting them that it's okay. You also run the risk of waiting so long to talk with the person about it, that when you finally do, it's been weeks or even months since it happened, and the person is left confused as to why you're finally bringing it up. Be prompt and direct in addressing behavior that is unacceptable. It's better for everyone. But just because you address something right away, that does not mean the problem will be solved instantly. Don't look for quick fixes of resolution and fall into the trap of instant gratification. Instant gratification is your enemy! If you have issues, leadership needs to roll up their sleeves and get to work.

Speaking of getting to work, this also applies to hiring processes. You can look for months trying to find someone whom you think can help with a quick fix, or you can hire someone with great parallel experience that can be applied to your company and teach them how to run your specific business. When you make a hire, you (the leader) should roll up your sleeves and teach that new team member the ropes. You'll not only be providing an immediate knowledge base to your new hire, but you'll also be role modeling for everyone in your company the exact behaviors needed. When you do this, you end up building a team that can help you branch out other team members from it. If you're looking for someone else to do the hard work for you, your problem is deeper than just needing that one quick hire.

3
TOXIC POSITIVITY

A research study in 2006 was performed in an effort to measure the psychological differences in people who were asked to either suppress or accept their emotions. They did this by having them watch an emotionally engaging film, and monitoring their heart rate, breathing, and overall stress levels after the film. And guess what? The participants who were asked to suppress their emotions had a higher stress level after the film. They also concluded that suppressing emotions negatively affects social adjustment and general well-being. Three other studies have also shown that suppressing emotion lowers self-esteem.

Why am I talking about suppressing emotions? Because now it's time to talk about toxic positivity. This may sound contradictory, because how and why could positivity ever be "toxic"? What does that even mean? How could positivity be bad? Well, in short, too much of anything—even if it's good—can be bad. Or, perhaps more appropriately, the wrong or untimely application of anything, however great it might be, can be harmful.

You may recall hearing about people who became extremely ill and even perished from drinking too much water in water-drinking competitions. They essentially overdosed on water. It's called water intoxication. That's right—the water became toxic. The fact that water is essential for life and is so healthy for us does not negate the fact that it can also be very bad for us. Similarly, positivity, when misapplied, can be toxic too.

When talking about workplace culture, negativity and toxicity are always a hot topic. What you do not often hear about, however, is Toxic Positivity. Toxic Positivity is when an employee's concerns are brushed off in an overly positive way, invalidating their opinion and making them feel small or insignificant. Essentially, you're belittling someone by being overly positive. This frequently occurs when concerns are pushed back on, denying that anything negative has happened, thus minimizing the person (or people) who have raised the concern and making them feel like their concern is invalid.

Toxic Positivity is something that should be shared and spoken about frequently. Identifying this will only help your business succeed by having a truly comfortable and inclusive environment for all. When someone comes to you with a concern, listen thoroughly and acknowledge the issue, even if it does not seem concerning to you. The issue was raised for a reason, even if you cannot see it, and that issue is valid because this is what the employee is experiencing.

Employees must feel like their concerns matter. How can they feel heard and appreciated when the issues they raise aren't taken seriously? Each member of your team is an integral part of your business operation. Everyone must have a voice and their voice must matter and make a difference. In this, it allows everyone to be equal.

When it comes to voicing opinions and concerns, everyone should be on the same playing field. Think of the myth of the Knights of the Round Table. You know, King Arthur and his knights. Do you know the significance of the table being round? It was to signify that everyone had equal say. A standard rectangular table has a "head" and a "foot". The person who sits at the head of the table is in charge, while the second in charge occupies the opposite end, with all other guests at the places in between them. But at a Round Table, there is no head or foot. Each place at the table is equal to the next.

You need to think of your business communications hierarchy as a Round Table. No one's concerns are more important—or less important—than the next. Instead, you are one cohesive unit, all comprised of unique individuals, each one with their own voice. Taking an employee's concern seriously and being attentive shows that person just how important and valuable they are to your organization. When workers feel valued, they provide even more value. So, start looking at how you "minimize" employees' concerns. If you try to throw a positive at them to brush it off, rather than discussing their concerns seriously, you're hurting them and hurting your business. Additionally, some leaders use Toxic Positivity to manage their own employment stresses. They can't handle the responsibilities of the position they have and as a result, fluff off extra demands and conversations by being toxically positive, thus freeing up more of their own time to try and meet personal goals. Dig down and discover if this is you.

4
YOUR D.E.I. PROGRAM NEEDS A MENTAL HEALTH CHECK

In 1963 the Equal Pay Act was signed into law, requiring equal pay to be given to men and women for equal work. The very next year, Title VII of the Civil Rights Act passed, prohibiting discrimination based on race, color, sex—including sexual orientation or gender identity, religion, and national origin. In 1990, the Americans with Disabilities Act was signed to protect the disabled in the workplace—which also extends to mental health conditions.

Diversity, equity, and inclusion are immensely important in the workplace. It empowers employees and shows customers your company promotes fair opportunities for everyone. Above all, it displays integrity, and who wouldn't want to work for or give their business to such a company? Having people of different backgrounds and opinions is the building block to having a strong DEI culture. But this isn't limited to ethnic background or physical disabilities, nor is it limited to employees in non-leadership positions. A proper DEI program includes leaders with mental health disabilities as well.

In a study by Pew Research Center in February 2023, it was found that over half of the employees agreed that DEI in the workplace was a good thing. Additionally, 61% stated that their company adhered to fair hiring practices. While the majority agreed

Counterproductive Culture

with DEI in the workplace, it was interesting to see the levels of agreement rising the younger the employees were. For example, workers under age 50 were more likely to agree that diversity in the workplace was very important to them. While it would be nice to have all ages on board equally, one cannot deny the growing awareness and importance of DEI.

Even though people with disabilities are often overlooked when it comes to DEI, the good news is, according to the same study, about half the employees said it was very important for them to work somewhere that is accessible to people with disabilities. Most people, however, imagine these disabilities to be physical and forget that there are disabilities you cannot see. Here is where the efforts and importance of focusing on Mental Health as a part of your DEI programs come into place. You see, everyone suffers from some type of mental struggle. Even if it's something as "simple" as stress. Stress is indeed a mental health issue. Did you know that 90% of companies state they have a DEI focus within their organizations, however only 4% of those companies state they focus on mental illness and disability. That's a staggering statistic, especially considering that most employees suffer some type of mental challenge. Even if you think you don't, you really do. Remember, even something as "simple" as stress is a mental health challenge.

What does your workplace do to make positive impacts on the mental health of its people? Does your workplace even have a focus on positively impacting mental illness? Do you have representatives in place who struggle with mental health challenges leading and opining on all your meetings? Probably not. Most employers completely miss the mark here. You see, mental health wellness is one of the top reasons people quit their jobs. Having mental wellness focus programs is an extremely important part of having a workplace that is dedicated to Diversity, Equity, and Inclusion.

A true DEI program must focus on not only diversity of ages and ethnicities, but also those with physical and mental disabilities. If you fail to, you're missing out on a tremendous wealth of information that can improve the way your company performs.

5

STOP LOOKING FOR SERVANTS

"We're looking for servant leaders!" But what exactly does that mean? Most importantly, what does "servant leadership" mean today? Its definition has remained the same, but the perception of it has changed dramatically and it's become an extremely negative term.

Servant leadership was once used to describe people who put the needs of others first, focusing on the growth and well-being of everyone surrounding them. While customers are still looking for great people who are pleased to serve them, there are a lot of groups who have forgotten the meaning of servant leadership. Servant leadership has transformed into a term where companies and leaders are looking for people they can exercise authority, power, or control over rather than to serve others together.

Under this new distorted meaning of the term, leaders are looking for easy-to-manage, easy-to-control employees who will not push back and will "stay in their own lane". Employers who look for this want to have complete control and power over their employees.

Francesco R. Benzo

"Little Silvio – Servant Leadership"

Counterproductive Culture

A good leader should lead—whether by example, instruction, or both. Those who manage in a style looking for others to serve them like to delegate, micro-manage, and control. Most importantly, companies and management who are looking for "servant leaders" to "serve" them are looking for "yes men" and "yes women". Leaders like this never want to be questioned, challenged or disagreed with. They want someone who will obey every single order that's barked out and will obey with a smile. Seeking servant leadership also means you're looking for people who do not think, do not push for more, and do not try to grow. This is a way that weak leaders surround themselves with people who will never have an opportunity to take their jobs!

If you're looking for someone to be a "servant leader" for you, you're just looking for a "servant". The term "servant leader" itself is ridiculous. Servants are there to do only that, serve people. They are never leaders of other people. The term "servant" itself should never be used to describe anyone or anything within your company.

Servant leadership has become an extremely negative term that all companies should stay away from using.

6

THE FISH ROTS FROM THE HEAD

Toys 'R' Us, the once iconic and booming toy franchise, declared bankruptcy in 2017, and then again in 2018. While many hypothesized this was because they simply couldn't keep up with online retailers such as Amazon, the real reason goes quite a bit deeper. Remember, the first problem you see is not the root cause of the problem.

To compete with Amazon, Toys 'R' Us first tried to adopt a similar strategy of allowing customers to shop online. But their delivery service was poor, and they did not match Amazon's low prices. While mirroring a more successful company's business model might seem like a good idea, in this case, Toys 'R' Us would never be able to beat Amazon at their own game nor should they have even tried. What they should've done was focus on what they *could* provide that Amazon couldn't—an amazing in-store, all-inclusive, all-immersive shopping experience with top-tier customer service! Part of the Toys 'R' Us allure was that the giant store both encapsulated and captivated you! When you were inside of a Toys 'R' Us, your mind turned off to everything else and only focused on the fun experience they provided. But Toys 'R' Us, like so many other companies, declined because of poor management.

Shortly after declaring bankruptcy, the company was approved to pay 16 million dollars' worth of bonuses to their top executives.

Counterproductive Culture

How can a bankrupt company approve bonuses to the leadership that put them into bankruptcy?! It's ridiculous! Surely, this bonus wouldn't have been approved unless they were hitting their company goals and getting back on track, right? Considering however that the company would declare bankruptcy again shortly after, shut down all 735 of its stores by June of 2018, and remove 33,000 employees from the workforce tells you a much different story. It appears instead that these bonuses were not a sign of success but the "big wigs" paying themselves off with little regard to anyone beneath them. They had no care for the families that were being affected and this once glorious company that changed so many childhoods became a rock to squeeze every dime out of.

Imagine if even a fraction of that $16 million went into a new marketing campaign or resources to build a new company brand more fitting with the changing retail landscape. Aside from that $16 million in bonuses, corporate leadership received additional millions in bonuses during the four-year period prior to the bankruptcy. What if a little time and effort went into creative strategies to keep their brand alive by improving the in-store experience? Now here we are, a handful of years later, and Toys 'R' Us is making a comeback, based on the in-store experience!

Have you ever heard of the expression, "A fish rots from the head"? You might be asking what that even means and why we're talking about fish, but bear with me.

"A fish rots from the head" is a metaphor for companies and organizations that fail because of their leaders' poor decision-making.

The role of a leader is so important that having the wrong person at the helm can be devastating. What's more, the bad habits of the manager will often trickle down to their direct reports, creating a ripple effect of bad influence. Soon, the entire workplace becomes stagnant and dysfunctional. This also ties into our previous discussion about people who look for "servant leadership". You see, a servant will never tell their boss that their head has begun to rot!

Leaders are responsible for guiding their enterprise to success. With this, we can equate such a leader to a pilot flying a plane. A company, after all, is only as good as its leadership, and the person in the cockpit greatly affects whether the flight makes it safely to its destination. Just like a flight can't be successful without a competent pilot, a business cannot thrive without good leadership. The diligence, work ethic, and positive company culture leaders bring to their teams are absorbed by the employees who work for them. All of those positive behaviors are then passed directly to the customers. Conversely, all of the poor behaviors are also passed directly to the customers.

Counterproductive Culture

Some of the easiest ways to be a great leader and keep your head from rotting are:

- Just be nice.
- Treat everyone with respect.
- Apply all rules and policies - don't play favorites.
- Consistent communication about the positive and the opportunities.
- Treat everyone equally.
- Follow through on all commitments and promises you make.
- If you screw up, say so! Apologize and get it fixed! Don't make excuses for the mistake or poor decision you've made. Learn from it and make yourself better.
- Don't be greedy.

Of equal importance is to acknowledge the people who make it happen. Everyone enjoys being rewarded and recognized, especially after a long path to achieving goals! Rewards and recognition, however, may not be plentiful enough to spread around to everyone in your employ.

Everyone has top performers they count on. What everyone may not do is dig deep into finding out who drove that positive performance. Who put the gas in everyone's tank? Who's work raised the bar that set everyone else in motion to reach those higher levels? Who provided the motivational spark that lit a fire under everyone to do great things? When you are looking to recognize and reward, find the spark. The spark is where it starts. Don't overlook it. No great fire ever started without a spark.

Remember, as a leader, you set the tone for your company's morale, culture, and ultimately, success. Instead of spreading rot, exude a contagious aura of positivity, fairness, and growth. Who wants to do business with rotten people, anyway?

7

IS YOUR APRON DIRTY?

It was the grand opening of a prestigious steakhouse, and Emily sat at a table and waited for her date. Inside the bustling restaurant, claps and cheers erupted around her. She looked around to find that the owner was making his rounds, going around to different tables and asking the patrons how they liked the food. The sweat on his face clearly indicated he had been working hard in the kitchen with the rest of the workers, and Emily thought it was so wholesome that even the owner would work right alongside his cooks and servers when he clearly didn't have to. She smiled, watching the restaurant owner wipe sweat from his face with the towel that draped around his shoulders.

When her date, Jeff, arrived, he sat down beside her, clearly excited about something. "Guess who I saw?" he asked.

"Guess who I saw?" Emily asked at nearly the same time. "You go first," said Emily, curious and puzzled.

Jeff settled into his chair. "I saw the restaurant owner," he said, shaking his head as he squinted. "Yeah, a car dropped him off at the back door of the restaurant. He dumped a bottle of water over his head and then rushed inside. So weird."

Emily smiled as her mind reeled at the possible explanations, and she was surprised and disappointed when the answer finally crystallized. He had faked it. The restaurant owner had dumped water on his face to make it look like he was sweating. He snuck through the back door of the restaurant, and then came out of the kitchen to greet the guests as if he had been working alongside them the entire time. His apron wasn't really dirty, but he had pretended that it was.

Is your apron dirty? This is a new time and a new era. Everyone is on social media, and everyone constantly posts pictures of what they're doing with their teams. Social media has given us the opportunity to celebrate everyone publicly with an immediate audience. If you look closely, however, you can tell what companies have great leadership and what companies are just sharing pictures to go through the motions and are faking it, just like the restaurant owner in our story. Keep in mind, this story doesn't just apply to restaurants. It applies to everything.

Did you get your clothes dirty helping everyone achieve that goal or did you just show up after the work was done and take a quick picture with your staff so you could look good? This is especially important at the executive level and above. Remember the story about the Vice Presidents in charge of looking out the window? They never got their suits dirty, and now, they are all gone. If your apron isn't dirty, you're not being a role model. You can choose to stand back and watch everyone as they work or, at some point, you can choose to get involved and help everyone with that work. If your apron is dirty, you've just created a spark that will result in your team matching your efforts every single day. So, ask yourself right now, how dirty is your apron today?

8
WORK HARDER, I WANT MORE!

In 2008, married couple Jason and Melissa left Microsoft and began writing a tell-all book about the horrors of working for the company. Four years later they would release *Stack Rank This!: Memoirs of a Microsoft Couple,* detailing the culture of overwork and burnout they faced working at the tech behemoth.

You see, Microsoft had a review system called "stack ranking". The stack ranking system compared workers to see who had the highest metrics. Even if the team succeeded as a whole, only a few select employees would be rewarded with higher pay and bonuses, thus pitting the workers against each other. As a result, everyone would overwork themselves in an attempt to reap the rare rewards of a bonus or pay increase. This stack ranking system encouraged overworking and burnout. It was the reason Jason and Melissa chose to leave their jobs—and then write about it.

The number one cause of this type of culture is greed. It's not because of short staffing. Short staffing many times is a result of an employer making a conscious decision. Money is being made by running employees hard and not having to pay additional salaries to be at an appropriate staffing level. Short-staffed or not, overworking will always lead to burnout.

There is a difference between saying you're doing everything to achieve a proper working culture for employees and doing it. The first sign of a "work harder, I want more" environment is short staffing.

Chic-fil-A is busy because they staff their stores one employee per position and, sometimes, two employees per position!

Customers know they can get their service quickly and properly. Companies that try to increase their bottom line by running with a skeleton crew and having that crew work harder are sending themselves backwards. Regardless of your business, the fewer employees you run with, the fewer people those employees will be able to serve. At some point, your customer volume will be managed down to a level that your reduced staff load can handle, regardless of your business. People can only go so fast.

You can't "save" your way to better sales. You must take care of your guests by staffing enough employees who can help them.

If you find it difficult to keep great employees, then you need to ask yourself some questions:

- What type of environment are you fostering?
- What is the condition of your facility?
- How does your pay compare to similar positions in the area?

Your facility doesn't have to be brand new, but it should be clean and in good condition. Maintenance and the impression of maintenance at your business will impact your reputation with guests as well as your employees. Poor maintenance also means your employees must work harder to get the job done.

If your pay and compensation packages are within 5% of your competitors', then you have a great shot at not only attracting candidates but keeping them too! If your pay gap is 10% or lower than competitors, your application inbox will remain empty. Who can afford to work for you at $54,000 when your competitor next door is hiring at $60,000? That's $115 more per week that employees can earn just by walking across the street and working for your competitor. $115 may not seem like a lot to some business owners, however, to an employee, that can help pay a lot of bills and keep them in their homes. Keeping that manager at $115 more per week, however, could certainly have a positive impact on your business.

What positive effect would running with increased staffing levels have on your management teams? Would you be able to attract more talent? Would you be able to have more motivated talent from within? Would you be able to keep talent longer and lower turnover? Good people aren't hard to come by. They are created by fostering positive environments that provide support and appropriate levels of workload for the role. Good people will take care of your business if you take care of them. Good people will also leave should you keep forcing them to work harder to achieve lofty goals.

9

IT'S OK, YOU CAN TELL US

As an employer, do you really want your employees to tell you flat out what they're experiencing or, do you prefer they comfort you and hold back their concerns? When you ask an employee why they're leaving a job, do you really want to know? Are your employees afraid to tell you about their experiences working for you? Do they fear retribution or being tagged as a problem? Ask yourself these questions. I am sure the answers may surprise you.

A better question is, could you handle the truth even if they told it to you? Or would their confession reveal a problem with your organization—a chink in your company's armor? Are you confident enough in your culture and operations to hear the truth from your employees? I hope so.

Going back to the "Round Table" example, when employees feel they are on equal ground to speak up and communicate clearly, your business will be better off for it. A company that has open and clear communication will always go farther than one that doesn't. Your business, and the employees who run it, will be much better off if everyone is encouraged to speak their minds. This will also allow ideas to develop as your idea-makers will be nurtured by this atmosphere of open communication. What will result are innovative employees and a strong company culture.

Counterproductive Culture

Imagine a company where employees are not encouraged to be honest, leaders don't want to hear the truth, and no one really communicates. The employees are afraid to approach management, and the leaders don't really want to be approached in the first place. They are always "too busy" and "short on time". How will the company grow? How will issues be resolved? This cyclical pattern of non-communication will create a toxic workplace in no time. If leadership is not available or willing to talk about issues, the employees will start to talk about the issues among themselves, and the atmosphere will turn into a miserable place where no one wants to work. The leaders in this type of environment will twiddle their thumbs, avoid issues, and sweep things under the rug like we've already talked about.

Telling employees they can always speak to you and actively listening with appropriate action are two different things. You must listen and then respond in a professional way that helps the employee understand why you can or can't take action on what you were just told. You should show them their honesty is appreciated by implementing changes to address their problem. Make the time and truly listen to any employee. They will lay out on the table their experiences in your company. Those employees who are not afraid to tell you what's happening and how to fix it must also be invited to be on your leadership teams! As an employer, you should always want someone to tell you in respectable detail what they have been through. Their open communication tells you that they will not hold anything back and not hide one thing from you. And isn't that the type of communication you want?

In allowing a truly open environment that is retribution-free, you are allowing your employees to keep their integrity and beliefs, resulting in an extremely strong working environment.

10

TO BONUS OR NOT TO BONUS?

Work here: $2,000 sign-on bonus! Wait, $4,000 sign-on bonus! Wait, we are still short-staffed, make it $8,000! Sign-on bonuses are great but not the best thing to hang your hat on as a way to attract employees. You're just throwing money away.

If you're going to compensate someone to join you, put it in their salary rather than dumping it on them as a one-time sign-on bonus. The best question is, how did so many employers go from giving employees a hard time over minimum wage increases the last few years, to now throwing tens of thousands of dollars out as a hiring bonus to every single employee? Think about it. The logic is ridiculous, and it's centered on greed. If you paid your employees a slight bit more than the minimum to start with, fewer of them would be leaving you. If you are paying competitive rates as compared to those around you, there really is no need for a sign-on bonus *if* you're a good employer with a positive reputation. There must be some balance on both ends of the scale and right now, that scale is broken. Furthermore, if you're giving out a sign-on bonus to new employees, what are you doing for existing employees who never received one? Ask yourself that question. I guarantee your existing employees have been asking themselves this and are waiting for your response.

Too many places have their priorities wrong. People should always be #1. Without people you have nothing. Simply pay your employees a higher wage, treat them with respect, give them breaks accordingly, don't ask them to work all day for you, and *pay them* for working extra when they do. It's very easy to be a great employer if you truly want to be one. You would expect these things for yourself so why do you think your employees don't expect them, too? The double standard is obvious and has become so clear it's funny.

Another funny thing is when someone quits, and you give them a raise to stay. They are leaving. They perhaps don't like you or your company anymore. Your solution is to buy them with a higher salary? I'll never understand why some companies choose to do this. Pay your people while they're working with you and reward them immediately for their achievements. Never make someone feel that they cannot grow or earn anything higher with your group. If you limit them, they will leave.

Now, back to that sign-on bonus program. If you have a sign-on bonus program, here are some things to think about and why you may not want to do it:

1. While you're giving hefty sign-on bonuses to new hires, are you giving the same level of bonuses to the employees who are already working for you that may not have received a sign-on? If you aren't taking care of the people already there, don't expect them to stick around very long. The sign-on bonus for new hires will increase turnover with your existing staff. Your existing employees will be very unhappy should they not receive anything, especially since they have been going through the trenches with your business.

2. A sign-on bonus is a clear message to customers that you're short staffed. Many businesses even put signs up all over their property announcing it. That sign stuck in the front lawn that says "Join Us" or "Now Hiring Go Getters" is uncomplimentary to your business. They look cheap and silly, especially when they aren't even placed well. To many customers, these signs are a sign to stay away.

3. You are much more likely to secure employees by paying them a higher wage than with a sign-on. While a bonus is nice, most people work for their guaranteed paycheck rather than the lure of a potential bonus. If you have a great sign-on but the pay is on the lower end of the spectrum, those folks may very well leave anyway. Everyone is paying more right now, having a sign-on does nothing for you unless your base pay and total compensation is at the top of the competitive range. If not, you're just making a bad investment by trying to throw money at the fire. Remember, the first problem you see is not the root cause of the problem. Throwing the wrong money at short staffing will not resolve it.

4. Employers have FOMO (fear of missing out). Just like surveying employees, sign-on bonuses have become something that everyone does just to say they're doing it, too. If you lure someone into working for you because of the sign-on bonus, what's to say that person won't be lured again by another group's sign-on?

Get your employees by being a great employer, with an impeccable culture, excellent pay, benefits, and a real focus on work-life balance. If you undercut any of these things, you'll need far more than a sign-on bonus to attract people. The employees working for you should be rewarded more than the new employees coming in. They are the ones who will speak positively for you as the representatives of your business, and they will ensure you don't need a sign saying so.

11
YOUR HR IS DISRUPTED

David took a sip of his coffee and squinted at his computer screen as he read the email from his HR manager. "Due to some employees not punching out for their scheduled lunch breaks every day, we will be implementing a policy where your lunch break will be automatically deducted even if you do not take a lunch." The email itself didn't bother him as he always clocked out for his scheduled lunch. No, there was another problem. In his state, this was illegal.

The above anecdote is a true example of what can happen when HR departments either aren't aware of, or simply don't follow laws while they attempt to be innovative or progressive—also known as "disrupting or "hacking" your HR.

HR, as we know it, was born out of desperate need following severe employee unrest in the late 19th and early 20th century. The first of what we would call an HR department was the National Cash Register Company's personnel management department in the early 1900s. Later, in the 60s and 70s, such personnel management evolved into human resources. While the need for competent HR is obvious, it seems some companies have gone overboard with trying to make their processes so efficient and progressive that they cut corners. This leads to breaking local, state, or federal laws, and contributing to a toxic work culture. Cutting corners never works. You cannot work your way around the stated rules and regulations of employment practices.

Remember when we talked about employees being protective-motivated? Well, the HR department does the same thing. If you think your HR department never makes a mistake, think again. In fact, they make far more mistakes than you think! Many times, in poor judgement. It's often that they attempt to protect themselves from failure and cover up for mistakes such as rushing investigations that turn out to be incomplete, cutting corners of standard filing practices, or engaging in otherwise detrimental behavior, including wrongfully terminating employees. As a rule of thumb, you should have an outside company come in several times per year and perform a complete audit of your HR department and its practices. This will ensure your company is compliant and up to date. Think about it, your field teams are constantly evaluated, inspected, graded, and surveyed while those in HR never experience a single check. How are you protecting your business if you don't have as many checkpoints with your HR department as you do with your other teams? Don't be surprised to find that your HR department is failing you, even if unintentionally.

There has also been a lot of HR talk going around lately about how to "fire" people. Some groups even specialize in telling you how to do it quickly! I find that disgusting and your employees will too. Your HR department should focus on how to educate and keep your people, not terminate them. Terminations shouldn't be a topic that is looked at in a celebrity light as they currently are. There is no secret way to "hack" or "disrupt" your HR process. The bottom line is the best HR departments are the ones that follow every single federal, state and local law pertaining to employment practices and are frequently

Counterproductive Culture

evaluated by outside sources. Your HR department professionals need to put their axe away and stop hacking. As a business leader you must put a system of external checks and balances in place to monitor your HR department for complete compliance. They will be better for it and so will you.

12

COACH TO IMPROVE, NOT REMOVE

It was early July in 2019 that Deutsche Bank in Frankfurt, Germany, let go of nearly 20,000 employees. They trimmed their workforce down to a fifth. The layoffs were concentrated in New York and London. While this may sound extreme, considering the numbers, it is not at all unusual.

In the United States, it's quite common to let go of thousands of employees at a time. Even amid a strong economy, mass layoffs have been shockingly regular. Verizon Wireless let go of over 40,000 employees in 2018, and even GE parted with almost 15,000 in a three-year period. Google laid off 12,000 in 2023 and from 2022 to 2023 Amazon laid off 27,000 workers. While these sweeping layoffs might make the news for a day or two, they don't seem to be remembered for very long. Everyone goes back to their business, and those who lost their jobs are forced to figure it out on their own.

For those people who suddenly find themselves without work, a trial of uncertainty, and often, financial difficulty awaits them. While their careers are placed on hold, their bills do not similarly pause. Rents, mortgages, and utility bills keep stacking—not to mention simple but necessary obligations like their phone bill or the cost of food and groceries.

It doesn't help that nearly 80% of Americans already live paycheck to paycheck and, as I'm writing this, the average wage an

Counterproductive Culture

American needs yearly to live "comfortably" is just under $100,000. Imagine suddenly losing your job when you're relying on the upcoming paycheck to pay your rent. Additionally, studies show it's much harder to get a job when you're unemployed—and gets harder the longer you're jobless. This makes the situation even worse. But perhaps even more importantly, albeit overlooked, losing one's job can be devastating to your self-esteem. This dramatically affects mental health, their careers, and a person's overall life.

Despite all this, eager layoffs are a very modern sickness. Mass layoffs were seen for the first time in the 1970s, and now, they've happened so often we've come to accept them. But should we?

A Guardian article in 2014 stated that most American companies wanted to run "lean and mean", no doubt alluding to increasing profits while being overly aggressive in managing costs. But what kind of work culture are you developing when you run a company that way? What message does it send to the employees?

When the temptation to lay people off arises, I propose a different solution. Work with the people you have. Instead of examining how layoffs might save you money, build up the people you have to become more productive. You see, most of these companies we've spoken about above who laid off tens of thousands of employees also went out the very next day hiring people to fill many of those same roles. Take a look at the job boards. Those same companies who cut back staff always have active postings to hire for the same positions they just had to "reduce". What many of these very successful companies are actually trying to "reduce" is the average employee pay and not necessarily the number of employees they have. They fail to recognize the cost of replacing an employee far exceeds the cost of keeping one. This is another reason you should *coach to improve, not remove.*

Check in on your employees to see how they're doing. Remember happiness improves business metrics, so well-paid and satisfied employees directly improve profitability. Coaching to improve, not remove is applicable for both layoffs and performance-based terminations. Before you start taking someone down the road to termination, step back and realize that absolutely no one always does everything correctly. No one can operate at 100% capacity all the time. Even robots have a fail rate. Additionally, you've no idea what challenges someone may be facing, yet they still showed up to work for you. Think about the mistakes you've made where someone gave you a chance to learn from them. Think about the harshness of the actions you're about to take on your employee and the family members attached who will also be affected negatively by your decisions. It takes time to learn. Time equals experience. Don't be critical. Don't be cynical. Be kind yet direct with the individual and give them every opportunity to succeed.

Still, there will obviously be times when layoffs or terminations may be inevitable, and when that is the case, I urge you to do it the right way. As we have discussed, losing one's job can be devastating, do not add to this by going about layoffs or terminations in an inhumane way. Do unto others as you would have them do unto you.

Counterproductive Culture

SHH, YOU'RE FIRED

"I know it's only an hour's notice, but I need you to stay late today." "I know it's only a day's notice, but I need you to cancel your vacation." "I know you are short-staffed, but I need to take two of your managers because the other district is short too and they aren't as strong as you are." "I know it's your day off, but I need you to come in."

"Quiet Firing" is forcing an employee to quit by treating them poorly or neglecting them. Tactics of this management style could be refusing to give someone a raise, not promoting someone who deserves it, or even continuously asking an employee to come in early or stay late. The entire idea behind quiet firing is to make the employee want to quit, and it's a cowardly way of handling terminations.

Be upfront with your employees. Firing is never fun, but your teammates deserve honesty. They are people with lives and aspiring careers, and being honest about a termination may help them develop, grow, and do better in their next role. Being sneaky and deceptive by quiet firing undermines the integrity of your organization. Worsening workplace conditions to get rid of employees is simply disgusting. Think of how you'd want to be treated in such a situation. Also consider the confusion an employee goes through as their workplace becomes worse and worse around them, wondering if they should quit but hesitant to do so because they need the money. As such, quiet firing is the equivalent of playing mind games with your employees. It's bad enough for you to terminate someone so why mess with their head on top of that? It's a childish way to try and achieve a result. Don't forget, if your company is doing this, at some point, you may be included in that drop list, too.

Furthermore, imagine an employee blaming themselves when they don't get a pay raise, when they get passed over for a promotion, or whenever else they are mistreated or neglected. Perhaps the employee's mindset is "I must work harder—I have to do better", when in reality, the employer has already made up their mind they don't want that employee working there anymore, and there's nothing the employee can do to change it. Essentially, the employee is going through turmoil for nothing. Try as they might, their performance will never be good enough, and they will be subject to mistreatment until they can take no more. Does this sound like a good way to treat anyone? If it does, think about it happening to you. Now how do you feel?

What do you do as an employer that provides a more professional, transparent environment for your employees? When it's time for terminations, do you approach this difficult task honestly and directly, or do you hide behind quiet firing because you're not brave and professional enough to sit face-to-face with the person you're about to damage? If you can't have a professional conversation with the person you're terminating, it means you've done something wrong to that employee and terminating them is covering up for your shortcomings. It's a hard statement but it's true. Why else would you have to sneak around trying to get someone to quit? Or why would

Counterproductive Culture

you have to treat someone poorly and speak to them with anger and negative emotion if you're terminating them? It's all the same and I sincerely hope you treat your employees with the dignity and respect they deserve.

Francesco R. Benzo

13
HE WHO HAS THE GOLD MAKES THE RULES

In 2019, Keiran arrived in Qatar, excited to start a new job at Al-Jazira Security Services. Although it wasn't quite the crime scene investigator job he had dreamed of as a boy, the job paid enough to earn a living and support his family—and that's all that really mattered. Or was it?

His salary was going to be 1500 Qatari Riyals per month, and Kerian was excited for the opportunity. But his hopes were dashed quickly by 12-hour shifts, no days off, and, worst of all, weeks of unpaid wages. Three months passed and he had only received just over 500 riyals.

The issue with Al-Jazira Security Services, as it is with other companies, was an entitlement that suggested employees must endure whatever hardships they deem necessary for the promise of future pay, because *He who has the gold makes the rules.*

These "rules" for Keiran included long shifts, not a single day off, and eventually, sleeping overnight in the company building. The idea that a worker must do whatever is demanded of him just to keep his job is as unfortunate as it is ludicrous. And, far too common, unfortunately.

If Keiran had not written about his struggles online in a post that eventually went viral, this behavior from the company would have likely continued. While Keiran was hesitant about speaking up for fear of retaliation, it was only because he decided to do so that things finally improved. Sadly, in most cases, the plight of the employee goes unheard. This is an unacceptable situation that far too many employees are made to endure, and it all stems from a false sense of entitlement that many employers hold.

Unfortunately, conditions like these exist in many countries. From the early 1800s through the 1900s, American workers dealt with long hours and low pay, unsafe working conditions, lack of job security, poor living conditions, and even child labor. This overall lack of workers' rights eventually led to the formation of labor unions and movements fighting for better pay.

Over a hundred years later, it is unacceptable that some of these practices are still alive, albeit in a slightly different form. Even in recent years, American workers have been mistreated by the companies they work for—all because the leaders of these companies feel they can do what they want. In 2022, for example, Barbara Smith, who worked for Amazon, realized her check was $100 short. As a single mother with a child, that $100 was quite significant. She wrote an email to the wealthiest man in the world, her company's owner, expressing her frustration with being behind on bills due to this mistake.

The New York Times would soon collaborate with Smith on an investigative piece that suggested this issue with shortchanging employees was widespread. And this wasn't the first allegation of mistreatment at Amazon. A previous piece by *The New York Times* alleged something darker—that Bezos held a theory that the longer an employee works for a company, the more complacent they get, and that it's more productive for a business to replace workers as time goes on. The idea was that new employees work harder. And the numbers didn't lie with a turnover rate of 150%, much higher than most companies. But how could a company be so emboldened to mistreat its employees to the point of convincing them to quit? Because they have the "gold".

It was even alleged that Amazon would pay resignation bonuses to encourage employees to quit. "Take this gold and be on your way"! But is "gold" really the all-important commodity that employers hold over their employees? Does having the "gold" dictate that you can do basically anything?

It should be clear that this is no way to run a business. It should be remembered that happy employees are always the most productive, and miserable, poorly treated ones will not stay long. Instead of having the attitude of "My employees must do whatever I want them to do because I pay them", employers should instead be thinking, "I should treat my employees with kindness and respect because my company does not exist without them". Similarly, employers should not convince workers to be okay with hardships because it's "part of the job". No one should ever need to "earn their way in". Once you've hired them, that means they've earned it. Too often employers use terms such as "this is a hands-on job" to encourage mindless overworking and discourage certain people from attempting to gain employment. Guess what? *Every job is a hands-on job.*

Counterproductive Culture

Don't try to convince your employees that mistreatment is simply a part of the job, or that the difficulties you're facing will make them better workers. Instead, be honest about it. "We work hand in hand with our people and do spend a lot of time on our feet however, we follow every single employment law out there and treat our people well." This is a far different approach in giving employees a statement about your workplace functions versus "this is a very hands-on job". Very hands-on is a blanket statement that can go in any direction. I've seen this statement used in places where you don't get to take your own meal period, never have a chance to sit down once or can barely use the bathroom but once a day if you're lucky—or shall I say, approved to use the bathroom. "May I use the bathroom?" "Not right now it's the middle of lunch service period, can't you hold it?" Using this statement is like going to the doctor with a dart stuck in your head, but instead of removing it, he encourages you to keep living life as normal while he runs some tests and drains your insurance for every dollar it has.

Francesco R. Benzo

Little Silvio – Opportunity Knocks"

Counterproductive Culture

Do not assume that since you pay them, your workers should be willing to do anything and everything for you, especially at the sacrifice of their own health. You should not demand your employees do whatever you want simply because you're the one cutting the checks. Companies should not feel they can require extra working days with no notice, extra duties or responsibilities with no compensation, or that they can call employees at any time of day they want, even when it's the employee's day off. Instead, treat your employees with respect, and realize although they may need you to earn money, *you need them* to do the same.

"He who has the gold makes the rules" refers to the exploited leverage companies hold over their employees because they are the ones who pay them. This type of poor behavior that some leaders put unto others is about greed and getting blinded by power, thinking that because you are paying an employee, you essentially own them and can do whatever you want, when you want. That's a very strong statement, but it's very true.

While it's technically true that employers have the "gold", that does not mean employers should have absolute power over their employees. Think about the California goldrush in 1848, when 300,000 people flocked to California to get their share. But that gold still had to be found and harvested by panning and digging. So, while employers indeed have the "gold", that gold is obtained by their employees who make the company successful with the work (digging) they do every day.

How well you treat the people digging for the gold determines how much gold they dig and the quality thereof. Gold doesn't find itself or dig itself out of the ground. Requiring your employees to be available 24/7 and work every weekend or holiday shows them you don't care about their lives outside of work. It also displays the selfish attitude of "he who has the gold makes the rules".

Do you think your employees are obligated to work whenever you want them to, just because you pay them? Have you ever reached out to an employee while they were on vacation to ask them a "quick question"? Or, even worse, have you asked an employee to come back early from vacation or denied their time off request, preventing them from going in the first place?

Your employees don't owe you every second of their lives just because they work for you. If you cannot treat them with the respect they deserve, they will eventually find a place that does. Instead of thinking "I have the gold, so I make the rules", I suggest you adopt a different mentality: "I have the gold because my employees help me acquire it." Your employees are valued team members who help your organization operate. Without them, you wouldn't have a company or business. So why not treat them that way?

Don't overestimate the power you think you should have over them, simply because you cut the checks. Be appreciative that there are checks to cut because of the people who are on the front lines working hard for *you*. It's very easy to be blinded by power when you have people working for you, but entitlement and greed are surefire ways to crumble even the strongest organizations. Respect your people and

Counterproductive Culture

their time. Those people will then give you more time, more people, and more gold.

14

WE'RE LOOKING FOR SOMEONE DIFFERENT

On October 2nd, 1954, Elvis performed at the Grand Ole Opry in Nashville, Tennessee. But after the show, Elvis was told by the concert manager that he didn't have any talent, and that he should go back to his previous profession, driving trucks. The concert manager, in charge of scheduling shows, had seen hundreds of singers and bands and, according to him, Elvis didn't have what it took to make it in show business. Now, obviously, he was wrong. Very, very wrong. But why did he think that? Did Elvis have an off night? Was the performance not very good?

A similar thing happens commonly in hiring, where an employer just doesn't see the job seeker for everything they possess and can offer. Just like the man who passed on Elvis, they believe they're looking for someone different, and they don't move forward in the hiring process because of that. Ask yourself, do your hiring managers really know what they're looking for?

Ever pass over a resume because the candidate only has 8 of the 10 "qualifications"? It's awfully cynical to think that person can't learn the other two missing things. Depending on what those two things are, maybe they can! Someone taught you, did they not? The answer is yes and is always yes, someone taught you the skills you've

Counterproductive Culture

developed today. This brings us to our topic.

Don't judge a book by its cover. Did you know that a tire company, Michelin, gives out the most prestigious food award in the entire world? The Michelin Star is awarded to restaurants with exceptional cooking. They strictly judge five criteria: quality of ingredients, flavor, cooking techniques, consistency, and even the personality of the chef expressed through the cuisine. A pretty thorough assessment for a tire company, right?

If a tire company can figure out how to recognize and reward the most prestigious chefs and eateries, even those based in gas stations, then the person on that resume you passed over can learn the other skills you need, if someone is willing to teach. Be a teacher. Choose to teach the missing skills to the right person. Everyone is so focused on trying to find someone who is 100% turnkey that they're losing out on great people who could just as easily turn that key with a bit of training.

As always, staffing remains the #1 issue in every single company. It's either you don't have enough staff or when you finally get staffed, the complaint is not enough "quality" staff. Just like your HR department, you should also audit your internal recruiting teams regularly. One very easy way of getting external sources involved with your internal recruiting team is to hire an external recruiting company to partner up and assist you. If you find the right group, there really are a ton of benefits that an external search firm can provide you regarding what's truly going on behind the scenes in your company.

The right firm can tell you who in your company is communicating and who isn't. The nature of communications. How are the interview processes going? What questions are being asked? What questions are not? How long are interview processes taking? How is training being performed in my company? Is training being followed? Most importantly, how is my new hire being treated?

External recruiting firms can do a lot more than just find candidates for you, if you're willing to listen to them. If you aren't working with an external recruiting firm, you're missing out on a great deal of added value and partnership benefits that can make dramatic improvements to your company. Maybe using a recruiting service hasn't been a fit for your company in the past. But as hiring platforms change, using a recruiter to help your business is something you should definitely be considering.

You see, there's no secret out-of-the-box, AI-automated, ultra-new, and modern way to hire people. No matter what method you use to attract candidates, it all comes down to interviewing the people who have expressed interest in working for you. If you can't make time to interview quickly, your candidates will disappear.

When you receive a resume, what do you look at first? How do those items you look at affect your thoughts on a candidate? I'd like to introduce a challenge exercise that every company should perform with every single employee, all the way up to the top, it's called **Block Out**.

Counterproductive Culture

With Block Out, go back through old resumes you've passed on and re-present them to your hiring management but this time;

Block out the candidate's name.
Block out their picture.
Block out the email address and social links.
Block out their physical address.
Block out the years when they were employed.
Block out the dates of their education and where their education is from.

Now all you have left to judge is the candidates' experience. Have your people review these *blocked out* resumes and tell you if they would like to interview those candidates or not and why?

How many more people would have received interviews with your company if all you had to view was a candidate's experience? I bet you'd have quite a few more people working for you, should you not have judged the book by its cover.

Francesco R. Benzo

ACCEPT MY OFFER!

Wonder why candidates don't accept your offers of employment or accept offers only to back out later? Here are some great reasons why:

1. A poorly conducted interview process. How many times do you make candidates come in for interviews, or how long does it take you to communicate with them and set up the next interview? Job seekers won't wait around forever. They expect a speedy process in scheduling and communication of interviews. Don't forget, your candidate is probably getting calls from several dozen employers, so acting fast is 100% necessary. The more organized and speedier you are in your process, the more the job seeker will think of you as a great potential employer and, the better it makes them feel!

2. Received another job offer. If you drag out your interview process, that job seeker, eventually, will get another job offer from someone else. This problem is reciprocal from issue number 1. The first problem you see isn't the root cause of the problem. The longer you take, the better chance an improved offer comes along from someone who acted quicker and showed the candidate they were wanted.

Counterproductive Culture

3. You took too long to call the candidate after they applied. It is always best to be the first company that speaks with a job seeker. If you think you can just schedule an interview when it's convenient for you, you'll lose out. Every candidate tries to interview with as many interesting companies as possible. Don't get caught up thinking everyone will wait for you.

4. Lowball offers. If you make a job offer that's underwhelming, you can expect that candidate to accept a counter from their current employer or an offer from another group they're speaking with. Even if they initially accept your offer, chances are it's going to fall through. A job seeker will almost never accept a salary offer that's the same or lower than what they're currently making, especially in this market.

Sending someone backwards on their salary is not a good way to show a job seeker that your company is the right place for them. It sends a negative message about your business and turns people off. If you really want that person to work for you, offer them a respectable salary that moves them forward, even just a bit, and makes them feel positive that you really value them. Also to note, offering a lower "training" pay with a promise to increase it after training is complete will also send a clear message to job seekers. Don't be cheap. If you hired the person then they deserve to be paid the full amount up front. Just as we said before, no one needs to "earn" their way in. You hired them, so, pay them. Don't nickel and dime anyone. You're losing far more dollars trying to nickel and dime than you think you're saving.

Francesco R. Benzo

WE NEED TO SEE YOU WORK

Another very interesting thing in hiring practices is the use of "On the Job Experience" or "Discover Days". For many years it has been a common practice that companies to do an "On the Job Experience" as a part of the hiring process. You bring your potential new hire in for a day or two and have them work a for a lower sum or even, have them sign a waiver with no pay. You watch them work to see if they can "hack" it and "keep up" with your business demands.

It seems that potential new hires for non-executive roles are subjected to this frequently. To a point, it can be helpful for you and the potential employee. Sometimes it does help ensure to the candidate that the type of work is something they are happy with and to also see if the employer's work culture is one they wish to be a part of. Why, however, do more companies not do an "On the Job Experience" for their most important corporate and executive roles?

Presidents, Vice Presidents, Regional Directors, Executive level staff, even Payroll, HR and office staff rarely are subjected to the same hiring experience that is required for candidates in those ground-level positions. Why would you not put them through the same type of working interview requirement? If you don't have everyone at all levels participate in some type of on-the-job experience, you've got a double standard going.

If you truly want to be an employer of choice and ensure you have the right people in place, it is a good idea to have an even and fair

Counterproductive Culture

hiring practice that is the exact same for all candidates your company hires, regardless of position or pay. Are the admin and executive roles not just as important as the rest? Of course they are! Why then would you not want to have those candidates perform the same type of working interview process as everyone else? Think about it. It's true and it will help you. Balance out your hiring practices and your people will respect you for it.

WILL YOU TAKE LESS?

Do you ask candidates "What's the lowest salary you would accept?" While you may be looking for the candidate to sell themselves more, the fact is they've applied to a position in which you've most likely had a posted salary range. Therefore, the candidate is looking for a salary in the range you advertised for said job. Asking them the lowest they would accept sends a ton of messages about you and your company. Your candidate will ask themselves, "What else may this company be doing through my course of employment to "cut back" or offer as little as possible?"

While you don't need to offer the candidate double their sum, you should always try and move someone forward in joining your company, even if it's just a little bit more than where they were before. This means base salary. Offering a candidate the same or less salary because you may have an increased benefit package is not forward movement. Benefits are always fluid. They can change any minute, be taken away or completely removed. If you're an employer, think about asking "What salary range are you looking for?" versus "What's the lowest salary you'll accept." In fact, stop being so coy! Just let your candidate know the salary range you have in budget and see if they are okay with it.

Negotiating salary doesn't have to be uncomfortable. Just cut right to it and make it work! The way you approach the salary conversation will earn respect from your candidates and open up professional negotiation or completely demotivate someone, causing you to lose them while they're still sitting in front of you.

WE NEED TO THINK ABOUT IT

"That person you speak with today and want to think about until tomorrow may be the same person someone else spoke with yesterday and will hire today." This is very simple and very true. If you're a business owner or decision-maker, think about the days when you were looking for a job and your experiences in doing so. Think about everywhere you applied while trying to get a job and how many times you were either passed over or, told someone would get back to you

Counterproductive Culture

"soon". Think about how many times they never got back to you and how angry you were about it!

If you find someone you like, it is guaranteed someone else likes them too. Do your due diligence but lock that applicant in with a set schedule of interviews, solid communication, and even a job offer contingent upon receiving or passing assessments your company requires. The more solid, tangible communication you put in front of your applicant, the better your chances are of keeping them interested in your company. The first problem you see isn't the root cause of the problem.

Take a deep dive into your hiring practices. What you are doing or not doing is really the cause of the problem. Even if you chose not to hire a candidate, get back to them and inform them they'll not be moving forward. Don't forget, *everyone is a customer.* You can and will earn a bad reputation with your customer base should your hiring practices, or lack thereof, make their way into the public.

Francesco R. Benzo

NOT TO BE PICKY, BUT…

We're looking for the "right" candidate. What is the "right" candidate? Is it someone whose experience or education matches your job requirements or, is the "right" person something else? Have you passed on a candidate because you don't like where they work? I'm sure you have. Maybe you had a bad experience there or know someone that worked for the company and didn't speak well of it. *Breaking news*, you should never pass on a candidate because you don't like where they currently work. That candidate doesn't' like it either and probably for the *same reasons* you have!

Does your "right" candidate have to live only 10 minutes away or, do you understand that a 45-minute drive, and sometimes more, is standard and really not that far to travel, especially if the position is in a large metro area where close housing may not be affordable based on the salary they will earn. How many years does your "right" candidate have to stay at a job before you consider them to have "good" tenure? Do you understand that tenure no longer means someone works 10 plus years at every role? Did you know that average tenure is rapidly decreasing to under 4 years at best? What exactly are you looking for, and how would you describe your hiring methods? Are you looking for a needle in a haystack? You'll find a needle once in a great while. But, while you're looking for that needle, don't forget you can build a lot of shelter with the hay you're pushing aside. What are you losing while you wait for the needle to be found?

Counterproductive Culture

Make up your mind because if you're never happy speaking with anyone or rarely decide that someone is a fit for you, there won't be anyone left to be found. Give someone a chance, just like you were given a chance. To get to a staff of 100%, you need to hire *one*. You can't look at staffing as a "big picture" item. Staffing and working with people are never "big picture". Working with people and building a team is about the "small picture". Every individual is their own picture, and all of those individual pictures are what makes the "big picture". Without the addition of *one*, the entire picture is amiss.

So, if you are trying to staff, start with one. Then, add another one! If you don't take the time to start with one, you will never get to one hundred percent!

WE CAN'T FIND ANYONE

Having trouble hiring? Don't forget, *everyone is a customer*. The reputation of your business can cause you difficulties when trying to hire staff. It can also help you hire staff should your reputation be positive. Keep your business clean, professional, and operating well within your community. If you don't, you'll have a very hard time convincing people to come work for you! Those Google reviews will say a lot about you. If you couldn't take care of them as a customer, how would you take care of them as an employee?

What's the best way to find great people? It's easy…be a great employer! Companies that always beat their chest and talk about how good they are to their people, most likely aren't. A great company shouldn't have to announce from the mountaintops that they are a good place to work.

If your company really is that great, your employees will announce it for you. Aside from treating your people well, you must offer a competitive and appropriate compensation package, have proper respect of their home life and, and display great leadership. Don't forget, leadership means listening, not lecturing. Start giving more chances and judging less, and I think you'll be pleasantly surprised. Some of the things you thought were missing in them might've taken just a little bit of development to show. No employee starts as a 10 out of 10, but many people can become a 10 for your organization if you're willing to invest in them and give them time.

15

CONTRACT YOUR WAY OUT

The use of temporary contracts as a testing ground for permanent employment has become a common practice. However, this approach doesn't always yield the intended results and can lead to unintended consequences. Oftentimes these contracts actually have a detrimental effect on both the employer and the employee.

Temporary contracts are often seen as a way to assess an employee's fit within a company before offering permanent employment. While to some it might seem like a logical step to test out a candidate's skills and cultural alignment before making a long-term commitment to traditional full-time employment, the reality is far more complex.

The first significant issue with this approach is that it fails to acknowledge the psychological impact it has on the individual. From day one of the contract, the employee will already feel uncertain about their future within the company. You must realize the message you're sending someone by offering a contract rather than traditional full-time employment. After going through the entire interview process, which may have also included assessments and background checks, you decide to offer a temporary contract instead of traditional full-time employment *because* you aren't sure about the employee! That's really the bottom line of it. You're telling that employee we really aren't sure about you but let's give it a temporary try. The first thing the employee does is question why they're not "good enough" for your role and then starts to feel insulted at the same time. Even with this, they may sign the contract as everyone has bills to pay.

Despite signing a contract, however, they are already exploring other job opportunities due to the lack of stability and security that comes with temporary arrangements. Also, in your failure to offer them traditional employment, they are now questioning *you*. In being overly critical, that employee is now critical of you as the employer.

Additionally, by relegating individuals to temporary contracts, companies risk losing out on talent who may seek out more stable employment elsewhere. In today's competitive job market, skilled professionals have numerous options available to them, and they are less likely to commit to an organization that does not offer a clear path to long-term employment or, questions an employee's viability in offering a temporary assignment contract.

Instead of using temporary contracts as a default method for evaluating potential employees, companies should consider alternative approaches that foster trust and commitment. This can include probationary timeframes, steppingstone results and several evaluation periods within a 6-month time. Contracts should be reserved for consultants who your company engages with to evaluate specific aspects of the internal business for short periods of time. This allows for targeted assessments without compromising the employee's sense of security.

Counterproductive Culture

Perception is reality. Many candidates will perceive a temporary contract as a negative connotation about them and about the leaders in your company who did not believe enough in the potential employee to offer a traditional employment opportunity. Employers should focus on creating a positive work environment that attracts and retains talent. Many times, these contracts also eliminate the possibility of health and other benefits too, leaving the employee to fend for themselves or having them search for an employer who will take care of these needs.

While temporary contracts may seem like a convenient solution for testing out potential employees, they often result in unintended consequences for both parties involved. Employers should rethink their approach to hiring and focus on building sustainable employment relationships that benefit both the individual and the organization in the long run.

Francesco R. Benzo

YOU'RE OVERQUALIFIED

Wait, someone can be overqualified? How is that possible?
They can't. Period. Saying someone is overqualified either means you're passing because someone is too "old" for you, or their money is more than you're willing to pay. There is no such thing as being overqualified.

You're hiring as you have a need. Would you rather hire the person who has never experienced what needs you're hiring for or, the person who has that experience and has been through every single thing possible, relative to the job you have open? That experienced person can make an immediate and positive impact which in turn, improves your business and makes your job easier.

Help make a change. If you're a business owner or person in management, encourage your people to bring candidates in that they are uncomfortable managing, like people who have more experience than they do. It will make them better managers for you, and you will have hired someone with excellent experience who will also make your business better.

16

PLEASE, HELP ME!

Emily sat, stunned, as she tried to process her mother's words. "That's your boss? I don't like him."

Truth was, Emily didn't like him either, but her mother had only met him for a second. What could she be picking up on? And why exactly did Emily not like him herself?

Her mother was always known for having keen intuition, and it was hard to ignore what she had just said—or her own feelings of animosity towards him. They were eating lunch together at her work's café, where her mother had stopped by to join her since she was in the area. When her boss spotted her eating on one of the benches outside the cafe, he came over to say hello. Instead of trying to figure out what her mother had picked up on, Emily chose to focus on her own feelings about her boss. What exactly did she not like?

On paper, her boss was nearly perfect. He led an extremely successful team, and he was always talking about his wife and children most warmly. Emily's mind reeled as she thought about what was bothering her. Finding no answers near to hand, Emily tried to ignore these feelings, and she finished her lunch, said goodbye to her mom, and went back to her desk.

But she couldn't stop wondering about what felt off, and soon, instances drifted into her mind, the frustration of those moments coming with them. After a recent switch in the CRM software they used, Emily had been baffled by the user interface. It was challenging to learn a completely new system after dealing with a different one for so many years. Other employees also faced the same difficulties. When she had requested help from her manager, she had gotten the cold shoulder.

"You'll work it out," he had told her. "You'll get used to it."

But what she had really needed from him was support, and that was nowhere to be found.

Her mind also drifted to the time when her boss was promoted. He didn't have a team meeting to discuss the changes, and he sent out a group email telling them they'd be on their own for a while during the period of adjusting to his new responsibilities. They had all tried to be supportive of this, but during the next eight months that followed, they received almost no help or guidance from him. Then it struck Emily like a bolt in the heart—her boss was simply not there for her. Or for any of them. He could not be counted on to help them.

In the world of leadership, one of the most critical yet often overlooked skills is the ability to make time for our team members when they reach out for help. It's easy to get caught up in the time crunch of daily deadlines and routines. True leaders, however, understand the importance of being available and making a few minutes for their employees when they ask for help.

There is a common pitfall to be addressed: the tendency to deflect requests for help by telling people to help themselves or referring them to company documents or online links. Oftentimes employees will also be referred to someone else on the "totem pole" and play the "chain of command" routine. While it may seem like a quick and easy solution, it often leaves individuals extremely frustrated and unsupported. It also quickly develops a perception in the employees' mind about the supervisor of their current company and how that company failed to provide support when asked.

When someone specifically seeks your guidance or assistance, they place their trust in you to provide meaningful support. Redirecting them elsewhere always comes across as dismissive and uncaring. This damages the trust and culture that everyone works so hard to build. If you can't take a few minutes to answer some simple questions, then what will you do when something big needs attention?

Another quick closeout is sending a brief email response and calling it "done". Depending on the nature of the issue, it will leave the individual feeling unheard and undervalued. Taking the time to engage in an actual conversation, whether face-to-face or over the phone, demonstrates your commitment to understanding the needs of the individual and showcases your ability to provide proper assistance that isn't passive or dismissive.

Failure to prioritize these interactions will lead employees to feel neglected or misunderstood. They will perceive it as a lack of care on your part or even as an indication that you're too overwhelmed in your own job to lend a few minutes. It's crucial to cultivate a culture of genuine support with your teams. You must make yourselves accessible and demonstrate a willingness to listen and assist whenever needed. By doing so, you not only strengthen your relationships with your colleagues but also create an environment where everyone feels valued and supported.

The next time a member of your staff reaches out for help, resist the temptation to offer quick fixes or redirect them elsewhere. Rather, take the time to actually help them and show you are truly walking the talk on the culture you claim exists within your company.

Counterproductive Culture

17

I.T. IS IT

It might be obvious to some that a brand like Tesla would understand the importance of the upkeep of technology to be more effective, but considering the company's success, I'm sure using this example doesn't hurt. Tesla didn't just use technology to sustain their business, they took it a step further and used it to drive sales.

So far, Tesla is the only car maker on the globe that uses software updates downloadable by Wi-Fi. That's right, no going into a shop or back to the manufacturer for system updates. Similarly, a person doesn't have to go to a dealership to buy a car—everything can be done online. And while other manufactures have now added some of these features, Tesla was the first one to do them.

Tesla also plans to use augmented reality to aid in the manufacturing process. As a smart vehicle, software, updates, and even games are melded into the vehicle owner experience through automated Wi-Fi updates. While Tesla was obviously exceeding expectations on the technology front, the bare minimum for a successful business is to ensure their information technology is up to date and working smoothly. I.T. is invaluable.

I.T. plays an extremely important role in the success of an organization. As the title suggests, "I.T. is IT". When your I.T. department fails, everything else fails like a stack of dominoes going down. It's a bold statement, but one that holds undeniable truth. Technology serves as the backbone of every business operation. From communication and collaboration to data management and customer service, the reliance on I.T. infrastructure is always at 100%. A minor glitch or a major outage will disrupt everything, leading to productivity losses, financial setbacks, and, most importantly, damaged reputations with your customers.

CLEAR YOUR CACHE, UNPLUG AND RESTART

Many times, there's a misconception that I.T. issues are always a result of "user error." While user errors can certainly occur, it's crucial for your I.T. professionals to approach every support call with an open mind and a readiness to investigate thoroughly.

Don't assume someone did something wrong! If technology was so trustworthy and bulletproof, we wouldn't need to keep resetting it all the time to make it work and we wouldn't need an I.T. department!

ONES AND ZEROES

First and foremost, I.T. professionals need to understand that they are dealing with people, not technology. When a support call is opened, it's a real person doing it. Too many times I.T. professionals treat people like "ones and zeroes". People aren't numbers.

The people making those calls are the ones making the money so, be good to them! Every call to the I.T. department represents a potential problem that could escalate if left unaddressed. It is imperative for all I.T. personnel to take every call seriously, no matter how trivial it may seem initially. Behind each call is a colleague or a client relying on your expertise to resolve their issue and keep operations running smoothly.

YOUR I.T. IS YOU

The way your I.T. department communicates with your employees is a direct reflection of your business. If your I.T. staff is passive, dismissive or rude, your company will have a bad name attached to it. If your I.T. department is welcoming, understanding, calming and comforting, your company will have a positive word of mouth as well as an increased employee satisfaction and retention rate!

The way your I.T. department communicates also dictates the type of communication they get back from your employees. If your I.T. department is complaining that employees are being rude to them, it likely stems from the I.T. department being rude, too. Think about it, why be rude to someone who is great to speak with and helps you resolve problems? People are rude to I.T. professionals when they aren't being helped in a friendly manner.

HOW FAST CAN YOU CLOSE A TICKET?

As with most companies, every call to every department is monitored for quality assurance purposes and timed for speed of resolution. But, sometimes, speed can get in the way of quality. I frequently order from the pet supply company, Chewy. They are very impressive in their shipping speed and ship out items the very same day. Oftentimes, however, they fail to properly pack the items, leading to damaged goods that become unusable.

It's clear that Chewy is fulfilling their orders very quickly, which most likely means their main focus is delivery speed, but they are falling short in product satisfaction. They are disappointing customers with damaged products and even being wasteful, as much of their product is food that pets can't eat when compromised. Having to throw out good food because it wasn't sealed properly is a regrettable consequence of rushing orders. If Chewy took just 120 more seconds

Counterproductive Culture

to properly pack and ship their items, they would have a lot more satisfied customers and far less waste with returns. Sure, their delivery speed might slow down a little, but what's a speedy delivery worth if the product that arrives is damaged?

Similarly, closing tickets out as fast as possible rarely leads to resolution, and the focus should always be on resolution rather than how fast something is closed. You must ensure that you've truly resolved the issue and provided adequate support before considering the case closed. This enhances and contributes to a culture of accountability and excellence within the I.T. department. It also enhances employee satisfaction as they can track open I.T. calls and see them as "in progress" rather than "closed", even though the problem is not resolved.

It's only natural that issues take time to resolve. Give each ticket your full time and attention and understand that faster is rarely better. By taking every call seriously, avoiding assumptions, and prioritizing resolution, you can uphold the reliability and efficiency of your I.T. infrastructure, contributing to the overall success of your organizations.

18

SURVEY SAYS!

I once had a doctor solicit me to do a positive survey for him. No joke! He actually said he needed help getting better scores! This led me to think about a common and unfortunate thing that happens in business workplaces—an extreme focus on numbers and data.

Over-surveying your people is one of those extreme focus areas that results in a *counterproductive culture*. Stop over-surveying your people. It's ridiculous. If you want to discover what is happening, make the time and take the calls from your patients, customers and employees when they come in. Most importantly, act upon those calls when you receive them. When people get to a point where they take the time and do a survey or post on their social media account about how poor the service was, you're way too late to fix anything. Surveys are a way of *reacting*, and sometimes there is a need for it, however, being *proactive* is to have a completely open door and answer everything as it comes in.

Don't put your customers or employees in the position that this doctor has been placed in. In a world of over-focusing and putting too much weight on surveys, this encourages rushed panic-working and takes away from true productivity.

Don't get me wrong—surveys are wonderful tools to have as a business owner in order to gauge successes as well as opportunities,

Counterproductive Culture

and they can give you valuable information. But watch out—don't get too caught up in them. The more time you spend looking at these reports, the less time you actually spend with your people.

It's your people who make the reports happen. Spend time with your people training and developing them. The harder you push to make the survey look good without role modeling behaviors for and with them, the more your people will go in reverse. Surveys and reports mean absolutely nothing if your people aren't getting results the right way. If you push them too hard, they will shut down.

I encourage all business owners who have been and still are over-consumed with dashboard reports and surveys to put them away and truly work hand in hand with the people working for you. Get results the right way. It will take longer but will put your business on solid ground.

Francesco R. Benzo

19

BE GOOD TO GOOD VENDORS

Apple Inc., famous for its state-of-the-art innovation and ubiquitous products, has developed a strong partnership with Foxconn, a main hardware producer in Taiwan. Foxconn is an essential provider of parts and supplies for Mac's iPhone, iPad, and other gadgets. This joint effort has empowered Apple to succeed by guaranteeing top notch items. While most people probably haven't heard of Foxconn, Apple would not be where it is today without them.

    I know you've heard of Walmart, but have you heard of Proctor and Gamble? Walmart, the world's greatest retailer, has built a close partnership with P&G, a quality manufacture for brands like Riches, Tide, and Pinnacle. P&G supplies a large number of family and household items to Walmart's stores all over the planet, making it possibly one of Walmart's greatest suppliers. Walmart and P&G have accomplished critical development and market predominance in the retail business. By utilizing each other's assets, they have effectively met the developing necessities to provide millions of customers with their retail needs.

    On the way to work, what coffee chain do you visit for your morning cup of joe? Starbucks? Starbucks and Starbucks Espresso Broiling Plants keep a good relationship with their espresso bean providers and espresso simmering plants around the world. These

Counterproductive Culture

connections are fundamental for guaranteeing a top-notch supply of espresso beans, which are the groundwork of Starbucks' items. Through direct partnerships with espresso producers, Starbucks has created a versatile inventory network to make sure their coffee keeps flowing.

Have you ever wondered how Amazon is able to deliver packages? Well, the answer is three letters: UPS. Amazon, the web-based business goliath, depends intensely on its partnership with UPS to deliver goods to clients around the world. UPS gives a range of delivery and strategies administrations to Amazon, including bundle arranging and transportation. This essential organization played a significant impact in Amazon's fast development and extension, empowering the organization to satisfy client arrangements rapidly and dependably. By partnering with UPS, Amazon has solidified its place in the worldwide retail industry.

On the other side of that coin, Nike, a worldwide forerunner in athletic footwear and clothing, fell under scrutiny during the 1990s and mid 2000s due to claims of poor treatment of assembly line laborers, a large numbers of whom were utilized by Nike's providers abroad. Reports arose of sweatshop-like circumstances, low wages, and other maltreatments in Nike's production network. These negative reports, which included Nike's treatment of dealers hurt its brand, and they even endured financial difficulties and legal hardships because of it.

Tesco, one of the greatest store chains in the UK, faced examination and regulatory assessment in 2014 following reports that it had purposely delayed payments to suppliers. This disturbed incomes and stressed connections with their vendors, and the outrage over this harmed Tesco's standing as a reliable colleague which brought about a huge decrease in its reputation and stock worth.

Treating your vendors with respect and kindness will always lead to more and better business in the future. Like your management teams and the employees who make your company run, your vendors are trusted partners who also help you grow and succeed. A company sells products or services, and without them, you have no business. These products and services are derived from your vendors. Simply put, you have no business without your vendors.

While this might seem obvious, you would be surprised how many vendors are overlooked, taken for granted, dealt with unkindly, or otherwise mistreated. The better partnerships you have with your vendors, the better products and services you may receive. On top of that, you will receive them more promptly and in better condition. It should go without saying that it's vital for your vendors to be treated well.

Every partnership involved in your business must be sound. We've spent a lot of time talking about the partnership between employers and the employees who work for them, but the connection you have with your vendors is just as important. Much like you wouldn't have a company without the employees who run it, you couldn't start or maintain a business without vendors. What's more, I think you'll find tremendous benefits in treating your vendors well, they will treat you well, too. Always treat your vendors as if the life of your business depends on their satisfaction, because it does.

20

DON'T LET THE GREAT BE THE ENEMY OF THE GOOD

Marylin Harper was excited to start her new job at a Home Warranty Call Center. After a two-week training period, she settled into her desk chair, hopeful about this new opportunity. She'd had tough jobs before, and tough bosses. She knew what it was like to work under strict metrics, and she didn't doubt for a second her ability to meet all the numbers required of her. She was never late to work, and she rarely called in sick. What's more, she was a hard worker, a fast learner, and she knew she was going to absolutely kill it in this new role. She was going to go above and beyond and be the best employee the company had ever seen.

"Five calls per hour," her cubicle neighbor said to her with a smile. "That's all you have to do. Well, you don't have to be perfect, but—"

"Oh, I'll get five calls per hour," Marylin cut him off. Just like she would never show up late, and just how she would work harder than anyone else. She would make sure she took five calls per hour, at the very least. And she did.

When a customer droned on too long, and Marylin needed to get them off the call to take the next one, she promised the customer to call them back so she could look into their issue. This went over well with the customer, as the thought of Marylin getting off the phone solely to resolve their issue sounded good to them. But Marylin was simply taking the next call to make sure she got in her five for the hour.

Soon, Marylin had a backed-up log of customers who were due callbacks but never received them. People began to complain, and even though she always took five calls in an hour, the service she was providing simply wasn't good. The reality was that, due to the nature of some calls, it wasn't always possible to take five calls in an hour without severely comprising quality of service. Although Marylin strived to be perfect, her method did not serve her well.

Perfection prevents profits. The harder you make the work, the less of it that will be done. Keep it simple. *Don't let great be the enemy of good.* Sometimes "good" is all you need. "Good" that is consistent. "Good" that can be maintained. Being perfect perpetually simply is not sustainable. Better to be "good" with a mistake here and there, than to be perfect for a short amount of time and comprise on quality or completely burn everyone out.

But it doesn't stop there. Doctors believe that perfectionism can lead to anxiety, depression, additional health problems and decreased productivity. So why strive for perfection when the health of your business—and your own physical health are at risk? We brought in 1000 guests today, but wouldn't it be great if we all doubled our time and brought in 2000 tomorrow? Yes, it would be great but, at what cost? Everything on this planet grew from a smaller idea into a larger one. And your business, similarly, can grow from a germinating seed—

Counterproductive Culture

watered with patience and consistency—into a sturdy tree bearing fruit. I hope you make that happen.

CONCLUSION

As we reach the end of this journey through *Counterproductive Culture*, I hope you find yourself not only informed, but transformed. The insights, strategies, and reflections shared throughout these pages are intended to ignite a deep and lasting change. A change in how you approach your teams, a change in how you manage your business, and a change in your personal leadership style. Whether you feel validated or challenged, inspired or introspective, the key takeaway is growth.

I am sure you've found new ways to enhance your workplace, celebrate victories and build upon them with your people. If you've identified areas needing improvement, embrace them with an understanding that they are opportunities and with every step you take towards positive change, it is a step in the right direction. The goal can never be perfection, but progress.

Remember, the true measure of success isn't only found in the achievements of today, but in the continuous pursuit of betterment tomorrow. Leadership is a journey, not a destination, and by committing to the principles in this book, you are investing in a future where your business and its culture will thrive.

Your willingness to learn and grow will set you apart as a leader who truly cares about the success of your organization paired with the well-being of your team. Keep striving, keep improving, and keep believing in the power of a positive, productive culture. I look forward

Counterproductive Culture

to continuing this journey together and hope you will join me in my upcoming book, *Exercises for Achievement.*

Here's to your continued success and the prosperous journey ahead.

Francesco R. Benzo

"Look in the mirror, leaders, see,
The root of woes lies in thee.
In your reflection, the true enemy,

You forge the culture, day by day,
In words you speak, in roles you play.

What you do and what you don't,
Creates employees' will or won't.

Your goals and demands so aspirant,
Makes your employees' can or can't.

Break the cycle, start anew,
With hearts and minds, not just the few.
Listen close, your team's in view,
Their wisdom vast, their passion true.

Empower voices, cultivate,
A space where trust can germinate.

With every glance in mirrored glass,
See the future, not the past.
In humble gaze, apologies should cast,
Your path to success will now be vast.

For ownership, the truth revealed,
In self-reflection's honest field.
A thriving culture, once concealed,
Now blossoms where the wounds are healed.

So turn the gaze from out to in,
Embrace the change, let growth begin." - *FRB*

www.ingramcontent.com/pod-product-compliance
Lightning Source LLC
Chambersburg PA
CBHW052206220526
45471CB00004B/1844